CULTURES OF THE WORLD
Moldova

Cavendish
Square
New York

Published in 2020 by Cavendish Square Publishing, LLC
243 5th Avenue, Suite 136, New York, NY 10016
Copyright © 2020 by Cavendish Square Publishing, LLC

Third Edition

Library of Congress Cataloging-in-Publication Data

Names: Sheehan, Patricia, 1954- author. | Quek, Lynette, author. | Nevins, Debbie, author.
Title: Moldova / Patricia Sheehan, Lynette Quek, and Debbie Nevins.
Description: Third edition. | New York : Cavendish Square, [2019] |
Series: Cultures of the world | Includes bibliographical references and index. | Audience: Grades 6+
Identifiers: LCCN 2019008222 (print) | LCCN 2019008281 (ebook) |
ISBN 9781502647511 (ebook) | ISBN 9781502647504 (library bound)
Subjects: LCSH: Moldova--Juvenile literature.
Classification: LCC DK509.56 (ebook) | LCC DK509.56 .S53 2019 (print) |
DDC 947.6--dc23
LC record available at https://lccn.loc.gov/2019008222

Writers, Patricia Sheehan and Lynette Quek; Debbie Nevins, third edition
Editorial Director, third edition: David McNamara
Editor, third edition: Debbie Nevins
Art Director, third edition: Alan Sliwinski
Designer, third edition: Jessica Nevins
Production Manager, third edition: Karol Szymczuk
Cover Picture Researcher: Alan Sliwinski
Picture Researcher, third edition: Jessica Nevins

The photographs in this book are used with the permission of: Cover FO Travel/Alamy Stock Photo; p. 1, 49 Piotr Velixar/Shutterstock.com; p. 3, 16, 51, 124, 129 Calin Stan/Shutterstock.com; p. 5, 84, 110, 127 alexandralarina/Shutterstock.com; p. 6 pavalena/Shutterstock.com; p. 7, 52, 114 Carsten Koall/Getty Images; p. 8, 85 Vadim Denisov\TASS via Getty Images; p. 9 Niall Carson - PA Images/PA Images via Getty Images; p. 10 Stanislav71/Shutterstock.com; p. 12, 34, 87, 100, 116 FrimuFilms/Shutterstock.com; p. 14 WildMedia/Shutterstock.com; p. 15 This World Photography/Shutterstock.com; p. 17, 66, 95, 105 Martyn Jandula/Shutterstock.com; p. 18, 39 Gagarin Iurii/Shutterstock.com; p. 19 mbrand85/Shutterstock.com; p. 20, 23 24 douglasmack/Shutterstock.com; p. 22 Nedelea Cristian/Shutterstock.com; p. 24 Popperfoto/Getty Images; p. 26, 29 TASS via Getty Images; p. 32, 38 VIKTOR DRACHEV/AFP/Getty Images; p. 36 Sandu Tarlev/Shutterstock.com; p. 37, 128 Serghei Starus/Shutterstock.com; p. 30, 40, 47, 64, 74, 77, 90, 97 DANIEL MIHAILESCU/AFP/Getty Images; p. 41 Dursun Aydemir/Anadolu Agency/Getty Images; p. 42 Janusz Pienkowski/Shutterstock.com; p. 45, 119 ungureanuvadim/Shutterstock.com; p. 46 Lee Hyoungho/Shutterstock.com; p. 48, 91 Igor Sirbu/Shutterstock.com; p. 50 Maxim Burkovskiy/Shutterstock.com; p. 53 aquatarkus/Shutterstock.com; p. 54 Sid0601/Shutterstock.com; p. 56 lmeleca (Leonid Meleca)/Shutterstock.com ; p. 57 Roveliu Buga/500Px Plus/Getty Images; p. 59 romeovip_md/Shutterstock.com; p. 62 Ali Atmaca/Anadolu Agency/Getty Images; p. 65 tomandy/Shutterstock.com; p. 67 jonnyslav/Shutterstock.com; p. 68, 75, 92, 108, 112 SlayStorm/Shutterstock.com ; p. 70 Cristina1994/Shutterstock.com; p. 72 pathdoc/Shutterstock.com; p. 73 Chumash Maxim/Shutterstock.com; p. 76 Constantin Mocanu/Shutterstock.com; p. 80 Irma Naan/Shutterstock.com; p. 82 Lumiere et compagnie/Shutterstock.com; p. 86 Natalia Vostrikova/Shutterstock.com; p. 88 MarinaNov/Shutterstock.com; p. 89 (top) Celso Coutinho/Shutterstock.com; p. 89 (bottom) RoD7/Shutterstock.com; p. 98 arogant/Shutterstock.com; p. 102 Iolanta Kli/Shutterstock.com; p. 103 Dmytro Larin/Shutterstock.com; p. 104 Alex_dobrii/Shutterstock.com; p. 106 Roman Belogorodov/Shutterstock.com; p. 107 Svetlana Bondareva/Shutterstock.com; p. 113 Veronica V/Shutterstock.com; p. 122 vvvita/Shutterstock.com; p. 125 Bas van den Heuvel/Shutterstock.com; p. 126 Ales Munt/Shutterstock.com; p. 130 RMIKKA/Shutterstock.com; p. 131 Fanfo/Shutterstock.com; p. 137 The Hornbills Studio/Shutterstock.com.

Printed in the United States of America

CONTENTS

MOLDOVA TODAY

N MANY WAYS, MOLDOVA IS A COUNTRY BETWIXT AND BETWEEN.
It's a part of Europe, but it doesn't figure much in the European imagination. Anonymous to the world and tucked away in southeastern Europe, Moldova is wedged between Romania to the west and Ukraine to the north, east, and south. The country is defined by rivers, but yet it's landlocked. It lies between the Prut (PROOT) and Dniester (NEE-ster) Rivers, which both empty into the Black Sea. That great body of water is not far from Moldova's southern border, yet the country lacks direct access, blocked by a small section of Ukraine.

Like Ukraine, Moldova was once a part of the Soviet Union. Communism ruled this former Soviet republic for fifty-one years, forever changing the lives of millions, until the Soviet Union fell apart in 1991. The collapse brought independence, but also economic decline and instability to Moldova. The small nation is still struggling to become a robust democracy, and is a work in progress.

It hasn't been a smooth road.

Officially, Moldova extends several miles across the Dniester to its eastern border with Ukraine. Unofficially, it doesn't. Already small in area, Moldova is

This map shows the official version of Moldova, without separating the breakaway republics.

further diminished in size by not one but two breakaway republics. One, Gagauzia, occupies four noncontiguous districts in southern Moldova, and functions as an autonomous region within the country.

The other is more of a headache. A long stretch of land on the eastern side of the Dniester River is the self-proclaimed republic of Transnistria. Politically backed by Russia, and bolstered by Russian forces, this part of Moldova wants no part of being part of Moldova. The people who live there are mostly ethnic Russians and Ukrainians who moved to the region during the Soviet years. Many of them, in fact, yearn for the old Soviet Union and run their affairs in the Soviet socialist manner. Moldova lacks the military heft to take on Russia, and following a short but bloody war and subsequent ceasefire in 1992, Transnistria remains a "frozen conflict."

Frozen it may be, but for Moldova, it remains a hot issue. The troublesome Transnistria is one of many reasons Moldova is having difficulty getting its feet on solid ground.

Instead, the small nation is being yanked this way and that like a rope in a tug of war. Mainly, the people tugging on that rope are the Moldovans themselves, as they search for stability and a clear sense of national identity. But they have plenty of help. Pulling in opposite directions are Russia on one side and Europe on the other. Adding muscle on both ends are conflicting loyalties to language, ethnicity, religion, history, the old ways, and the new. (In fact, Moldova even celebrates Christmas twice, on two different dates—New Christmas and Old Christmas—both of them official state holidays.)

Invisible but powerful players are also tugging on Moldova, and they include corruption, tyranny, and poverty. Moldova has the sad distinction of being the poorest country in Europe, while wealthy oligarchs hold much of the power. It's no wonder that Moldova is fraying at the edges and straining for unity.

The Democracy Index tracks the country's progress. The index, first published in 2006, is an annual report by the United Kingdom—based Economist Intelligence Unit that measures the state of democracy in countries around the world. Using a variety of indicators, its researchers assess a nation's electoral process, civil liberties, political culture, and government effectiveness. The resulting score determines whether the nation is defined as a "full democracy," "flawed democracy," "hybrid regime," or "authoritarian regime."

In 2017, the index lowered Moldova's standing from "flawed democracy" to "hybrid regime." According to the index, hybrid regimes tend to have the

A boy holds his dog at the gate in a poor district of Chisinau.

A woman votes in the 2019 Moldovan parliamentary election at a polling station in Chisinau.

following characteristics: "Elections have substantial irregularities that often prevent them from being both free and fair. Government pressure on opposition parties and candidates may be common. Serious weaknesses are more prevalent than in flawed democracies—in political culture, functioning of government and political participation. Corruption tends to be widespread and the rule of law is weak. Civil society is weak. Typically, there is harassment of and pressure on journalists, and the judiciary is not independent."

Another assessment group that does similar work is Freedom House. Its evaluation of Moldova in 2018 was on par with that of the Democracy Index. It classified Moldova as a "Transitional Government or Hybrid Regime" and assigned it the status of "Partly Free" (out of three categories: "Free," "Partly Free," and "Not Free"). It reported, "Moldova has a competitive electoral environment. Rights of assembly, speech, and religion are largely protected. Nonetheless, the pervasive corruption in the government sector, links between major political parties and vested economic interests, and deficiencies in the rule of law continue to hamper democratic governance."

Many Moldovans have been leaning toward Europe as the guide to democratic and economic success. Others believe they would be better off aligning with Russia and its allies. After all, their country was tightly bound to Russia for half of the twentieth century, and part of the Russian Empire in the nineteenth century.

Moldovans are proud of their identity, even as they dispute what that identity actually is.

Yet most Moldovans feel a deeper historical kinship with their neighbor Romania. They share the same ethnicity and speak the same language—though even *that* is a matter of dispute.

During its time as a Soviet Republic (1940—1991), the country (then called the Moldavian Soviet Socialist Republic) was heavily Russified, or Russianized. The Soviet Moldavians were forced to speak Russian. They were also made to believe that their native language, Romanian, really wasn't Romanian at all. Instead, it was nationalistically labeled Moldavian, and written using the Russian Cyrillic alphabet instead of the Latin alphabet used by Romania and most of Europe. That way, the two languages at least looked completely different. But the guise was only a grand deception aimed at breaking historical loyalties with Romania and forging new loyalties with Russia and its satellites.

Even today, some Moldovans will claim their language is Moldovan, not Romanian. This fascinating story of language confusion is emblematic of Moldovan identity in general. Who are the Moldovans and what is Moldova? The Moldovan people are still at odds over the answers to those questions. The rest of the world, meanwhile, takes little notice.

GEOGRAPHY

A fountain adorns a park in Chisinau.

MOLDOVA IS A TINY COUNTRY wedged between two much larger neighbors, Ukraine and Romania. Small as it is—only slightly larger than the state of Maryland—it is diminished in size even more by the two breakaway republics operating unofficially within its borders. Moreover, Moldova is landlocked because gigantic Ukraine reaches west and takes what small coastal area Moldova might have had if its eastern and western borders continued on their trajectories a few more miles south to the Black Sea.

What the country lacks in seacoast, however, it makes up for in rivers, which number some three thousand. However, most of them are very small waterways. But the Prut and Dniester are mighty rivers, and they flow along a good portion of Moldova's borders. The country sits between the Prut to the west and the Dneister to the east. It measures 217 miles (350 kilometers) long and 93 miles (150 km) wide, covering around 13,070 square miles (33,851 square kilometers). Moldova shares 279 miles (449 km) of border with Romania in the west and 583 miles (938 km) of border with Ukraine in the north, the east, and the south.

The Dniester River, Moldova's most important waterway, rises in the Carpathian Mountains in Ukraine. The river is navigable for about 750 miles (1,200 km), which includes much of its passage through or bordering Moldova. Shipping lines run from Soroca to Dubăsari in Moldova, and from there to the Black Sea. However, navigation is difficult on the lower reaches because of shallow water and sandbars.

PHYSICAL ENVIRONMENT

Moldova is an extremely fertile land with an average elevation of 482 feet (147 meters) above sea level. Its highest point, Mount Balanesti, stands at 1,411 feet (430 m). The country's topography is diverse, ranging gently from rolling, hilly plains in the north to deciduous forests and mountainous highlands in the center to a steppe zone in the south.

RIVERS

There are approximately three thousand rivers and streams in Moldova, and all of them drain south to the Black Sea. Only 246 of those rivers exceed 6 miles (10 km) in length; just eight extend more than 62 miles (100 km). Three river valleys running from northwest to southeast contain most of Moldova's towns.

To the east, the Dniester River forms part of the border with Ukraine and is navigable almost throughout the country. (The river goes by several names.

The Raut River cuts through a green valley in the rocky hills of the Orheiul Vechi region.

It's sometimes seen as Dnister, the Ukrainian name; or Nistru, the Romanian spelling.) The Dniester is an important traffic artery for the shipment of grain, vegetables, sunflower seeds, cattle and cattle products, and lumber, all of which are produced in the Dniester Basin. The Dniester swells during the rainy season and at the end of winter, when the ice starts to melt. If the winter is warm, however, the river does not freeze.

The Raut River, a short tributary of the Dniester, flows through a narrow valley in central Moldova. In the west, the Prut River divides Moldova from Romania. It's a tributary of the Danube, which it joins at the southern tip of the country. The Ialpug, the Cogalnic, and other southern rivers flow into the estuary of the Danube River in nearby Ukraine.

There are some 2,200 natural springs in Moldova. They are tapped for the country's water supply.

CLIMATE AND SEASONS

The country has a temperate continental climate. Average daily temperatures in the summer generally exceed 67 degrees Fahrenheit (19 degrees Celsius). Winters are fairly cold, with average daily temperatures ranging from 23°F to 27°F (-5°C to -3°C).

Conditions in the fall are changeable, with heavy rains in some years and droughts in others. Rain is heaviest in the higher regions, where it can exceed 21.7 inches (55 centimeters) per year. In the south, annual average precipitation is 15.7 inches (40 cm).

FORESTS

Forests cover about 12 percent of the country. Deciduous forests of hornbeam, oak, linden, maple, wild pear, and wild cherry cloak the steep hillsides of central Moldova, where the forested areas are called Codrii. Centuries ago, much of this part of the country was covered in forest, but clearing for agriculture greatly decreased the codrii.

A male roe deer sprints through a meadow.

FAUNA

Many kinds of animals flourish in Moldova. On the steppes, hamsters, hares, and partridges are predominant. The forest steppe is populated by wild boars, badgers, and wolves, among other animals.

Of all the deer species, the roe deer is the most common. Many other species of deer are no longer found in Moldova. To curb the declining numbers, some animal species have been introduced to the country. For example, the Kashmir deer was a local species that almost disappeared in the 1950s. Since then the Ascanian deer has been introduced to the Moldovan forests and reserves, as have the European elk and the Sika deer. Other imported species include the Siberian stag, the fallow deer, and the muskrat.

There are a rich variety of birds, both resident and migratory. Commonly found species include the hawk, the woodlark, and the long-eared owl. Along the rivers, ducks, wild geese, and herons can be seen.

The dwindling fish population is of great concern to environmentalists. The most common are perch, pike, bream, and roach. Some species, such as trout, are no longer found in Moldova.

CITIES AND REGIONS

The republic is divided into thirty-two districts and three municipalities (Balti, Chisinau, and Tighina). It has around sixty-six cities and towns, and more than 1,575 villages. Many of the villages are too small to have their own local governments, and administratively they are part of other cities or towns. The major cities include the capital city, Chisinau (kee-she-NOW) (formerly spelled Kishinev), with approximately 820,000 people; Tiraspol, with about 149,000; Balti, with 144,000; and Tighina, with 89,000.

A long-eared owl perches on a post.

Moldova also has two autonomous, or self-governing, regions—Gagauzia and Transnistria. Gagauzia is made up of four noncontiguous enclaves in the south of Moldova. Transnistria—sometimes spelled Transdniestria or called Trans-Dniester, and unofficially, the self-proclaimed Pridnestrovian Moldavian Republic—is a long, narrow strip of land running along much of Moldova's border with Ukraine to the east. It sits across the Dniester River from the rest of Moldova, hence its name, *trans-* ("across") *nistria* ("the Dniester"). It has ten cities and towns and sixty-nine smaller villages.

CHISINAU   Founded in 1420, Chisinau lies on the Ikel River in the center of Moldova. It grew rapidly from a small village into an important rail junction between Romania and Russia during the nineteenth century. Chisinau suffered massive destruction during World War II, when bombing and fighting destroyed more than 70 percent of the buildings. Most of the existing buildings date

from the mid-twentieth century, when the city was rebuilt. Main streets were widened, tall office buildings were constructed, and industrial parks were planned. Factories in the suburbs account for nearly half of all industrial production in Moldova.

Many shops are found in the capital, as shopping is a major recreational pursuit. The city looks like a typical Soviet provincial city—built on a rectangular grid with huge concrete, nondescript buildings. Along the main street, the monotony is broken with some neoclassical mansions—a reminder of the country's past. Since independence, the main street, formerly named Lenina after Lenin, has been renamed Stefan cel Mare Boulevard. Many other streets have also been renamed, in most instances to honor Romanians instead of Soviet figures. Great National Assembly Square, the main square, features a

A tram bus runs along the street in Tiraspol, in Transnistria. The Transnistrian State Drama Theater is in the background. The breakaway republic's red and green flag is easily seen.

triumphal arch built in 1846. Behind the square stands the Nativity of Christ Cathedral, recently restored, and a park.

The city is the center of arts in the country. It has theaters, an opera house, and numerous museums, such as the National Art Museum, the National History Museum, and the Archaeology Museum. A beautiful lake runs along the central park of the city, which is located near the state university. One of the city's most attractive buildings is the sky blue Ciuflea Monastery, built in 1858. It has nine dome-topped towers and an ornate interior filled with icons.

TIRASPOL The second-largest city in Moldova, Tiraspol is located across the Dniester River in the Transnistria region, where it serves as the capital of the self-proclaimed but unofficial Pridnestrovian Moldavian Republic. Like other

Eastern European cities, it endured heavy damage during battles between the Soviet Union and Germany. Its population consists mainly of Russians, ethnic Moldovans, and ethnic Ukrainians.

Founded in 1792, Tiraspol is now an industrial center well known for canning and winemaking. Other industries in Tiraspol produce farm equipment, footwear, textiles, furniture, and carpets.

BALTI   The largest city in the north, Balti lies on the Raut River. It is home to several of Moldova's major industries, such as winemaking, sugar refining, and tobacco processing. Fur coats, machinery, and furniture are also manufactured here.

TIGHINA (ALSO KNOWN AS BENDER)   One of the country's oldest cities, Tighina was founded around the second century BCE. Its Russian name is Bender, which means "belonging to the Turks," and it also goes by that name today. Tighina is situated southeast of Chisinau on the western bank of the

A view of Balti, which also goes by the name Beltsy, its Russian name.

Dniester River. Throughout history, the city has been attacked and occupied by numerous foreign powers. It has also been rebuilt many times following destruction in various violent clashes. In 1992 it was the center of fighting between ethnic Russians and the Moldovan military called the Transnistria War. Even though the city lies in the demilitarized zone that was established following that war, it is now controlled by Transnistrian authorities.

A medieval fortress is surrounded by cannons in Tiraspol.

Tighina is a manufacturing center for textiles, electrical equipment, and food. Silk made in Tighina is among the finest in the world. A seventeenth-century Turkish fortress still stands in the city as a reminder of the turbulent past.

INTERNET LINKS

http://www.moldova.md/en/content/geography
The official website of the Republic of Moldova includes a page on geography.

https://www.osce.org/magazine/211691
"Managing the Dniester" discusses the cooperative role of Moldova and Ukraine in caring for the river.

HISTORY

The military cemetery in Tighina (also called Bender) provides a resting place for soldiers from many countries and many wars, from the eighteenth century to World War II.

Though it has
many ancient ruins
and magnificent
old monasteries,
Moldova attracts
the fewest tourists
of any country
in Europe.

2

THE COUNTRY THAT IS TODAY called Moldova has existed in many forms, with different borders, and under different names over its long history. It has been subject to frequent invasions and foreign domination. Each era left a legacy, but Moldova has been influenced mostly by Russia, and later, the Soviet Union—which was primarily Russia. The imperial and Soviet governments tried to integrate Moldova's economy into their own and Russianize the Moldovan people.

For a long time, the plan seemed to work. Then, in 1991, the Soviet Union broke apart. At that point, Moldova declared independence and went its separate way. Independence was not a new experience for the country, as it had existed briefly as a sovereign state before, but this time there was much to undo from the previous regime.

EARLY HISTORY

The Dacians were the ancestors of the Moldovans. Numerous archaeological traces have been found, including burial places and religious cult constructions between the Dniester and Prut Rivers, dating to the fourth century BCE. Farmers who settled in the river valleys, the Dacians

The ruins of the fourteenth-century Neamt Fortress stand in the Moldavia region of Romania. The fortress provided a crucial defense position for Stephen the Great.

traded with the Greeks, who had established trading posts along the Black Sea coast.

The Romans conquered the Dacians in 106 CE, and the local population had to learn Latin. The Romans built roads, forts, and trading centers but eventually left the area for conquests farther afield. Slavs settled in their wake. In time, the Romanian language developed from Latin. Various nobles ruled the area, and one of them, Bogdan of Cuhea, founded the principality of Moldavia, which included the area known as Bessarabia (eastern Moldova). The first document referring to the land of Moldavia dates to 1360 CE. In 1391, ethnic Moldavians were mentioned for the first time.

MOLDAVIA AND THE TURKS

The most important figure in the formation of the medieval Moldavian state was Stephen III of Moldavia, also called Stephen the Great (reigned 1457—1504). He defended Moldavia's sovereignty in battles with the Ottoman Turks, the Hungarians, the Polish royal troops, and the Crimean khans. Fortresses from his time still stand. The medieval principality was, for much of its history, under Austro-Hungarian rule. A large part of Moldavia was later incorporated into present-day Romania and Ukraine.

During his rule, Stephen organized a strong force of peasants to resist the Ottoman sultan. On August 20, 1503, he signed a treaty with the sultan that managed to preserve Moldavia's independence, at the cost of an annual tribute (tax) to the Turks. Stephen was also a supporter of the arts and a religious crusader, and his architects built Orthodox churches throughout the country. In addition, he increased trade links with the rest of Europe and the Middle East. Stephen is remembered for maintaining a long period of stability in Moldavia. Today he is considered a national hero, and in 1992, the Romanian Orthodox Church canonized him (proclaimed him a saint).

After Stephen's death, Moldavia became part of the Ottoman Empire in 1513 and remained so for the next three hundred years. This was a stable period, but by the eighteenth century, the empire began to break up. Between 1711 and 1812, the Russians gained control of Moldavia five times. Eventually Turkey was defeated by Russia. As a result of the Treaty of Bucharest in 1812, which ended the six-year Russo-Turkish War, Moldavia became part of the Russian Empire. But this did not last very long. By the beginning of the twentieth century, western Moldavia had become part of the united nation of Romania. The eastern part of Moldavia, called Bessarabia, remained under Russian control.

A statue of Stephen the Great, or Stephen III of Moldavia (1433–1504), stands at the entrance to the park bearing his name in Chisinau.

WORLD WARS

During World War I, Russia suffered great damage. There were widespread food shortages, and people became disillusioned with the empire. Following the Bolshevik Revolution in 1917, a year before World War I ended, the Russian Empire collapsed. Bessarabia declared independence from Russia and united with Romania. A treaty was signed on October 20, 1920.

In 1922, the Russian communist leaders founded the Union of Soviet Socialist Republics (USSR), which included Russia, Ukraine, and several nearby republics. In August 1939, the USSR, led by Joseph Stalin, and Germany, led by Adolf Hitler, signed a treaty that banned hostilities between the two countries. The agreement allowed Stalin to annex certain territories. A year later the USSR occupied Bessarabia and renamed it the Moldavian Soviet Socialist Republic. Bessarabians who resisted Soviet rule were deported to Siberia or Kazakhstan, imprisoned, or killed. In one year, 1940—1941, nearly ninety thousand people were arrested and deported. Churches were looted and closed; many members of the clergy were killed.

Soviet troops parade before the population of Kishinev (now Chisinau), Bessarabia, in September 1940, after the Soviet Union acquired the province from Romania .

The nonaggression treaty between Germany and the Soviet Union lasted about two years into World War II, but Germany broke the pact by invading the USSR in 1941. Romania, allied with Germany, attacked Ukraine and reoccupied Soviet Moldavia from 1941 to 1944, when Soviet forces retook the territory.

SOVIET RULE

With the restoration of Soviet rule in 1944, large numbers of Russians and Ukrainians resettled in Moldavia, especially in the industrial centers along the eastern bank of the Dniester. Stalin decided that Moldavians and Romanians were now separate ethnic groups, even though the former had relatives across the Prut River in Romania. He insisted that the language the Moldavians spoke was not Romanian but Moldavian, and he imposed the Cyrillic alphabet used by Russians to replace the Latin alphabet used by Romanians. The intent of that was to break Moldavia's past connection with Romania, and to forge a cultural bond with Russia. And it had exactly that effect. Russian became the official language.

In 1950, Leonid Brezhnev, a Soviet official from Ukraine, was sent to Moldavia to ensure compliance with Soviet laws. Private farms were declared Soviet property, and government-run farms were under the direction of Russian and Ukrainian managers. The result, at first, was large-scale famine, leading to 115,000 deaths.

During the 1970s and 1980s, after becoming president of the USSR, Brezhnev continued the policy of Russification (Russianization). The Soviet government actively propped up the Moldavian economy, building industries and housing. More ethnic Russians and Ukrainians began to settle in Moldavia.

STRIVING FOR INDEPENDENCE

Moldova's gradual movement to independence sped up in 1986 with Soviet leader Mikhail Gorbachev's reformist regime and policy of glasnost, which means "openness" in Russian. As the Soviet Union started to relax its policies, a number of independent political groups in Moldova evolved, working toward national and cultural independence. The Popular Front of Moldavia, a political party, was formed, and pro-independence pressure intensified. This push was supported by mass demonstrations.

The leaders of Soviet Moldavia agreed to some demands, such as the use of Moldovan as the official language, and Romanian names replaced Russian names for major cities. Moldova's progress toward independence and reform accelerated after economist Mircea Druc was appointed prime minister in May 1990. The Moldavian parliament changed the republic's name from Moldavia to Moldova, adopted the blue, yellow, and red colors of Romania's flag, and issued a declaration of sovereignty. The following summer, some one hundred thousand Moldovans took to the streets demanding independence, and Gorbachev could do little to stop Moldova from leaving the Soviet Union.

AFTER INDEPENDENCE

On August 27, 1991, the Republic of Moldova officially gained its independence and became a sovereign state. The move was followed by the establishment

Demonstrators in Chisinau support the parliament's decision to declare the independence of Moldova.

of customs posts on the border with Ukraine. A Moldovan national army was also formed.

The first presidential elections were held in December 1991, and Mircea Snegur was elected president. Multiparty parliamentary elections were held in February 1994, and the communist-led Agrarian Democratic Party won the largest number of seats. A bloc of socialist parties came in second. Petru Lucinschi was elected speaker of the parliament, and the government was headed by Prime Minister Andrei Sangheli. The parliament passed a new constitution for the Republic of Moldova, and in April 1995 the first multiparty elections were held for local, self-governing bodies. Presidential elections were held again in 1996, where Lucinschi won a surprise victory over the incumbent Snegur, to become the country's second president.

As president, Lucinschi instituted some very controversial reforms. His tenure was marked by constant legislative struggles with Moldova's parliament. During this time, the country suffered political instability and an economic disaster brought on by a financial crisis in Russia. In Moldova, the standard of living fell quickly, and most of the population plunged into poverty. Hundreds of thousands of people left the country. In this climate, the Communist Party gained popularity.

SEPARATIST MOVEMENTS

The single most important political challenge facing Moldova after gaining independence was a lack of unity among its people. Two ethnic minorities resisted Moldovan rule and moved toward separatism. The first group lives on the eastern side of the Dniester River, in a region known as Transnistria, and is largely made up of ethnic Russians. The second group, in the south of the country, are the Gagauz people, a Christian, Turkic ethnic group that speaks its own language.

When Moldova became independent, these two groups were concerned about their future and the protection of their national and ethnic status. These concerns were based on fears that Moldova would unite with Romania, as regions of Moldova had historically been part of Romania. That idea was not far-fetched and is still being floated today. The Transnistrian Russians and the Gagauz worried that in such a case, they would be small, marginalized minorities in a large country that was ethnically and linguistically Romanian. These fears were exacerbated when Moldovan—which is essentially the same as Romanian—became the official language of Moldova. Russian speakers marched through the capital and walked off their jobs to protest what they viewed as increased discrimination. Many Gagauz do not speak Moldovan, and had similar concerns.

TRANSNISTRIA SEPARATISTS

Tensions between ethnic Romanians and ethnic Russians worsened in 1990. A political group promoting greater autonomy for the area was formed.

On September 2, 1990, Transnistrian separatists declared the region to be an Autonomous Soviet Socialist Republic called the Pridnestrovian Moldavian Soviet Socialist Republic ("Pridnestrovie" is the Russian name for Transnistria.) The Moldovan parliament immediately annulled the declaration. Violence erupted in November 1990 during elections for representatives to the Transnistria Supreme Soviet, or Parliament.

The conflict escalated in late 1991 following Moldova's declaration of independence from the Soviet Union. The leaders of the separatists then declared Transnistria's independence from Moldova. Fighting in the spring of 1992 resulted in many lives lost and considerable damage to the economies of both Transnistria and Moldova. This conflict is called the Transnistria War.

Meanwhile, the Soviet Union itself was experiencing its own difficulties maintaining unity. It dissolved at the end of December 1991, and its former republics—including Moldova—were granted self-governing independence.

A cease-fire between Moldova and Transnistria was declared in July 1992. The Russian Fourteenth Army, which has been based in the Transnistria region ever since, has acted as peacekeepers (or defenders of Transnistria, depending on the point of view). To prevent further bloodshed, the Moldovan and Russian prime ministers later signed a withdrawal treaty.

In 1995 the Russian president, Boris Yeltsin, acknowledged Moldova's territorial integrity, and the issue of Transnistria's sovereignty returned to the negotiating table. A signed accord guaranteed Transnistria's autonomy, but

independence was not granted. Nevertheless, Transnistria took matters into its own hands and held elections in December 1995, much to the displeasure of the Moldovan government. Igor Smirnov was elected president of the region; he held that office through 2011.

In May 1997, a memorandum recognizing Moldova's territorial authority over Transnistria was signed in Moscow. Discussions commenced for the drafting of a final document to govern the normalization of relations between Moldova and the Transnistria separatists. Yeltsin indicated that Russian troops would stay in the region until a settlement was reached.

As of 2019, the Russian army was still there. In June 2018, the UN General Assembly—which does not recognize the legitimacy of Transnistria—adopted a resolution urging Russia to unconditionally withdraw its troops from the Republic of Moldova, including Transnistria.

In 1991, in the city of Dubasari, supporters of Transnistrian independence confront advocates for integration with Moldova. The flags in the foreground feature the colors of Moldova and Romania. Dubasari lies in what is now unofficially Transnistria.

SOCIALIŞTII PENTRU
UNIUNEA VAMALĂ

SEMNEAZĂ!

ПОДПИШИСЬ!

СОЦИАЛИСТЫ ЗА
ТАМОЖЕННЫЙ СОЮЗ

PARTIDUL SOCIALIŞTILOR DIN REPUBLICA MOLDOVA

In Comrat, Gagauzia, activists put up a tent to gather signatures for union with Russia. The sign uses both the Romanian language, in the Latin alphabet (*top*), and the Russian language, in Cyrillic. Many of the Gagauz people speak only Russian.

GAGAUZ SEPARATISTS

When Moldova proclaimed its independence, the Gagauz people in the southern part of the country almost unanimously preferred to remain a part of the Soviet Union. In August 1990, they proclaimed their region to be an Autonomous Soviet Socialist Republic, but the Moldovan parliament did not recognize it. Soon enough, however, that became a nonissue as the Soviet Union dissolved.

The 1994 Moldovan elections marked the turning point in relations between the Moldovan government and Gagauz representatives. One particularly important issue for the Gagauz was the law which made Moldovan the only official language. As the majority of the Gagauz were not fluent in Moldovan, they were afraid that they would lose their influence in the country.

In 1994, Moldova granted Gagauzia (also called Gagauz Yeri) the right of self-determination and special legal status as an autonomous region. The region consists of three cities and twenty-three communes in four noncontiguous parts, with its capital being the city of Comrat. Gagauzia's official languages are Gagauz, Romanian, and Russian.

Under Moldovan law, the region remains part of Moldovan territory, and the Moldovan government determines its budget. A locally elected parliamentary assembly, governor, and executive committee act as the local government.

COMMONWEALTH OF INDEPENDENT STATES

In 1992 Moldova joined the Commonwealth of Independent States (CIS), an alliance of former Soviet republics, and gained a seat in the United Nations. The alliance with CIS helped Moldova acquire raw materials and provided a market for its finished goods, which was necessary after the Soviet Union ceased to exist.

There is constant tension between conservatives in the country who want to return to the old days of central control and liberals who want a restructured market economy. The strained relations between Moldovans and ethnic Russians and Gagauz in their autonomous areas continue, and while Russian troops remain in Transnistria, this remains a serious issue.

Although Moldova remains a member of the CIS (as of 2019), there are many in the country who would prefer to join the European Union (EU). A country cannot belong to both organizations at the same time. In 2018, Moldova stated it would not withdraw from CIS until it had formally applied for EU membership, which it expected to do in 2019. Moldova has already entered into several cooperative projects with the EU, including joining its Eastern Partnership in 2009. However, for Moldova to be admitted to the EU, it needs to achieve certain political and economic reforms and standards.

A 2017 poll found 60 percent of Moldovans favoring becoming a part of the EU. Neighboring Romania became a member in 2007. Ukraine was long a member of the CIS. However, Ukraine withdrew officially from the CIS in May 2018, after Russia illegally annexed Ukraine's Crimean Peninsula in 2014. (Russia stated it was merely helping Crimean separatists gain independence from Ukraine.) Similarly, the former Soviet state of Georgia quit its CIS membership

The European Union (EU) is a political and economic organization of twenty-eight European member nations.

Moldovans shout slogans opposing President Vladimir Voronin's "dictatorial leadership" at a rally in Chisinau in 2009.

in 2008 following a conflict with Russia over its breakaway republic of South Ossetia.

TWENTY-FIRST CENTURY

The political battles in Moldova between the Communist Party and the opposition parties have been based on whether the country should align with Europe and the West, or continue its alliance with Russia.

The Party of Communists of the Republic of Moldova, which had been banned in 1991, was legally revived in 1993. In the 2001 and 2005 elections, the Communists won an overwhelming victory. Moldova became the first post-Soviet state to return a non-reformed communist party to power. The Communists elected Vladimir Voronin as the country's third president in 2001.

In 2000, the Moldovan parliament changed Moldova from a presidential to a parliamentary republic. As such, the president was then elected by three-fifths of the votes in the parliament, and no longer directly by the people.

Although the Communists gained the greatest share of the vote again during the April 2009 elections, the other four parties combined secured a greater percentage of the parliament. That led to the formation of a coalition called the Alliance for European Integration. The day after the Communist victory, mass demonstrations took place in Chisinau, organized in part by the opposition parties. The protesters accused the Communists of election fraud, and the demonstrations turned violent. Three young people were killed. Both the government and the opposition accused the other of inciting the violence. Against this background, the parliament failed to elect a new president. The parliament was dissolved, with a new election to be held in July. In that election, the Communists lost to the pro-European alliance.

The new ruling coalition called a referendum in 2010 to return to the system of direct presidential election. However, the vote failed due to a lack of voter turnout. As subsequent parliamentary votes failed to elect a president, the country ultimately went three years without one. In 2012, the parliament finally elected Nicolae Timofti as president, with the Communist Party boycotting the vote.

In early 2016, a Moldovan Constitutional Court decision returned the country to direct presidential elections, reversing the constitutional amendment of 2000 that allowed the parliament to select the president. That year, Igor Dodon won Moldova's first direct presidential election in more than twenty years. The next election is to be held in 2020.

INTERNET LINKS

https://www.bbc.com/news/world-europe-17601579
This BBC News timeline covers major events in Moldovan history, with particular attention to the twenty-first century.

https://www.bbc.com/news/world-europe-18286268
This profile of Trans-Dniester (Transnistria) provides historical information on the separatist region.

https://www.britannica.com/place/Moldova
This encyclopedia includes a short overview of Moldova's history, with many links.

GOVERNMENT

A demonstrator wears the flag of Moldova on her back.

U NDER THE SOVIET SYSTEM, THE legislative branch of government was called the Supreme Soviet. On May 23, 1991, the Moldovan Supreme Soviet renamed itself the Parliament of the Republic of Moldova, which subsequently declared its independence from the Soviet Union.

In reality, becoming a new independent nation would not be as easy. While the collapse of the Soviet Union in 1991 brought great benefits to much of Eastern Europe, in Moldova it ushered in economic decline and instability. Substantial financial support from the Soviet Union (primarily Russia) had propped up Moldova for decades, but now it suddenly evaporated. Moldova has worked hard ever since to establish democratic political systems, but changing from a communist government to a democracy has been difficult. Charges of corruption taint each new administration, and contradictory laws keep changing the structure of the government.

Moldova remains the poorest in all of Europe. Young people continue to flock overseas to find work. There was a strong anticipation of change, but so far, it's dragging far behind expectations.

THE CONSTITUTION

The new constitution of Moldova, passed by the national parliament on July 29, 1994, defines Moldova as a sovereign state with a free-market

3

President Igor Dodon holds a press conference in Chisinau in 2017.

economy based on protection of private property rights and independent executive, legislative, and judicial branches of government.

Personal rights and freedoms are ensured according to the UN Universal Declaration of Human Rights. All citizens are equal before the law, regardless of ethnicity, language, religion, or political beliefs. The state guarantees the rights of political parties and other public organizations. In keeping with the country's ethnic and cultural diversity, the constitution enshrines the rights of all minorities and the autonomous status of the Transnistria and Gagauz regions. Administration of the cities and municipalities is based on the principles of local autonomy and democratic elections.

GOVERNMENT INSTITUTIONS

THE EXECUTIVE BRANCH This tier of government consists of the president (head of state), the prime minister (head of government), and a cabinet. The president is elected in a national election for a term of four years, and is eligible for a second term. He has broad powers and acts as the head of the military, with the authority to declare a state of military emergency, subject to parliamentary approval.

The president appoints a prime minister with the consent of Parliament. He leads a Council of Ministers that carries out the functions of government. The president must be over thirty-five years old, a resident in Moldova for at least ten years, and a speaker of Moldovan.

In 2016, Igor Dodon was elected president, and the next presidential election is scheduled for the fall of 2020. However, in 2017—2018, President Dodon was temporarily suspended several times by the Moldovan Constitutional Court for rejecting ministerial appointments and for refusing to sign legislation. At that time, the parliamentary chairman, Andrian Candu, assumed some of the presidential functions. How this turn of events will influence the 2020 election remains to be seen.

The prime minister is designated by the president upon consultation with Parliament. Within fifteen days from designation, the new prime minister must receive a vote of confidence from Parliament. In 2016, Pavel Filip was approved as prime minister.

THE LEGISLATIVE BRANCH This lawmaking branch of government consists of a directly elected parliament. There are 101 seats. Fifty-one members are directly elected in a simple majority vote by their constituency (body of voters in the area they represent). The other fifty members are elected from party lists on a proportional representation basis. The parliament has the power to adopt laws, approve the state budget, determine military matters, and exercise certain supervisory powers over the work of the government.

In February 2019, a two-part referendum was held in Moldova alongside parliamentary elections. Voters were asked to decide whether the number of parliament members should be reduced from 101 to 61; and whether a member of parliament should be open to recall. Both measures passed.

The Parliament Building in Chisinau.

THE JUDICIAL BRANCH

The court system has three tiers and is independent of the executive and legislative branches. Municipal and district courts are generally courts of first instance, with appeals first to an appellate court and then ultimately to the Supreme Court, the highest court in Moldova. There are also specialized courts with jurisdiction over economic and military disputes. The Constitutional Court, which is independent of other courts, has jurisdiction over all matters relating to the interpretation of the provisions of the Moldovan constitution. All judges serve four-year renewable terms.

NATIONAL SECURITY

Moldova's armed forces are under the jurisdiction of the Ministry of Defense. The national army includes land forces and air forces. Citizens between the ages of eighteen and twenty-seven were required to serve one year in the military. Although exemptions existed for medical or educational reasons, bribery was allegedly widely used to obtain those exemptions. In 2018, however, Prime Minister Pavel Filip announced that compulsory military service would be gradually abolished by 2021, as Moldova made the switch to a purely professional army.

Moldova spends very little on the defense sector. In 2018, only 0.3 percent of the country's GDP was allocated to the army. With such a small army, Moldova is well aware that it cannot defend itself against a major threat such as Russia. To bolster its security, west-leaning politicians have advocated joining NATO. Indeed, in recent years, Moldova has participated in various international military exercises with professional armies, especially those from NATO countries.

The chairman of Moldova's Constitutional Court, Dumitru Pulbere, speaks with the media in Chisinau on April 11, 2009.

Moldova's pro-Russian president, Igor Dodon, tried to block such initiatives by invoking the constitutional military neutrality of Moldova. But he was not successful, and the government deployed troops anyway at such military exercises. However, new elections might swing the national mood back to his way of looking at things. Time will tell. Meanwhile, Russian soldiers and Transnistrian troops in the breakaway region carried out more than two hundred military exercises in 2017 alone.

Article 11 of Moldova's Constitution states, "The Republic of Moldova proclaims its permanent neutrality. The Republic of Moldova does not allow the deployment of armed forces of other states on its territory." Nevertheless, as of 2019, some 1,500 troops of the Russian army unit called the Operative Group of Russian Troops (OGRT) remained stationed in Transnistria. In addition,

New recruits in the Moldovan army prepare to parade in Balti on September 21, 2018.

Russia also keeps four hundred peacekeepers there, purportedly to maintain the cease-fire that ended the conflict between Moldova and its separatist region.

The Moldovan government has repeatedly asked Russia to withdraw those troops and to transform the peacekeeping operation into a civilian mission with international oversight. Many of the Russian-speaking residents of Transnistria want the Russian troops to stay to protect them from being fully integrated into Moldova.

In January 2012, Moldovans protest Russian military presence in Transnistria. Several days earlier, Vadim Pisari, an eighteen-year-old Moldovan, was shot dead by Russian peacekeepers at the Vadul lui Voda checkpoint between Moldova and Transnistria.

INTERNATIONAL RELATIONS

Since Moldova gained independence on August 27, 1991, most foreign countries have officially recognized its independent status. Moldova is also a member of the United Nations (UN), the North Atlantic Cooperation Council, the

European Bank for Reconstruction and Development, the World Bank, and the International Monetary Fund (IMF). On July 13, 1995, Moldova became the first former Soviet republic to be admitted to the Council of Europe.

With the assistance of the United Nations Development Programme, Moldova has created programs supporting democracy, entrepreneurship, women in development, foreign trade, disaster mitigation, and sustainable human development. In addition, Moldova is a member of the North Atlantic Treaty Organization (NATO) Partnership for Peace program, the World Trade Organization, and the Organization for Security and Cooperation in Europe (OSCE).

Prime Minister Pavel Filip of Moldova (*left*) shakes hands with NATO leader Jens Stoltenberg at a meeting in Brussels, Belgium, on March 30, 2017.

INTERNET LINKS

https://freedomhouse.org/report/freedom-world/2019/moldova
https://freedomhouse.org/report/nations-transit/2018/moldova
These reports provide an overview of the state of democracy in Moldova, from the point of view of the watchdog organization Freedom House.

http://www.moldova.md/en/content/government
This is the official site of the Republic of Moldova.

https://www.newsweek.com/russian-soldiers-occupy-european -country-and-neighbors-are-trying-get-them-out-992855
This article examines the presence of Russian forces in Transnistria.

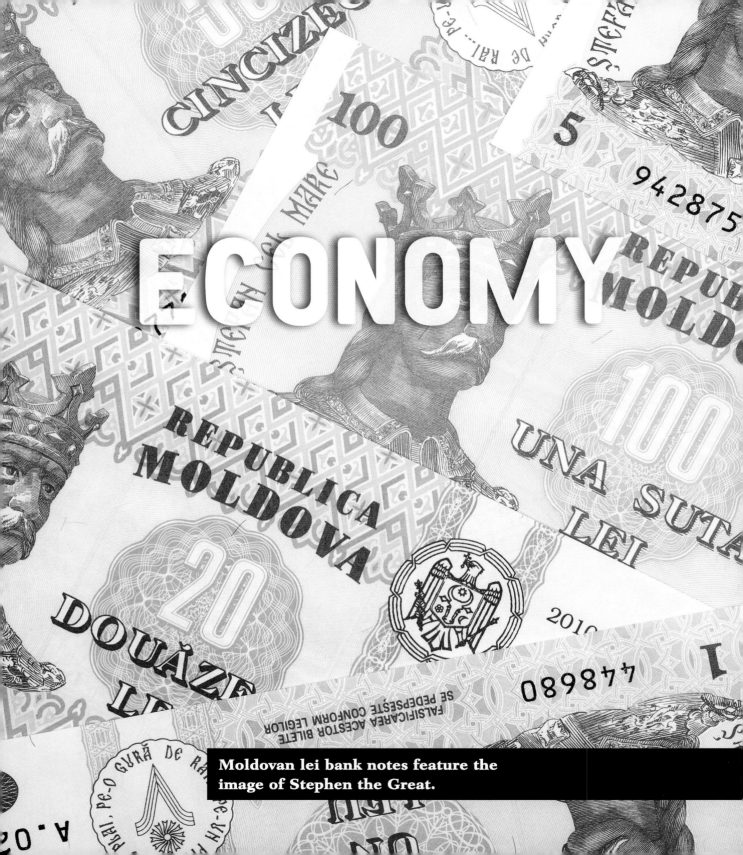

ECONOMY

Moldovan lei bank notes feature the image of Stephen the Great.

4

I N THE LAST TWENTY YEARS, MOLDOVA has made significant progress in reducing poverty and promoting economic growth. However, it remains the poorest country in Europe, and faces serious challenges. These include a precarious government and a very polarized society. At times, the government tilts toward Europe and the West, hoping to find new markets and economic ideas. But then a new, pro-Russia government sweeps in and changes course. The effect is like economic whiplash.

The breakaway, autonomous regions, particularly Transnistria, present unresolved problems that weaken the country's economic vigor and discourage outside investment. Although Transnistria covers only 12 percent of Moldova's territory, the region is of high economic importance for the country, as it straddles the major land routes to Russia and other strategically important export markets. In addition, most of Moldova's industry is located in Transnistria.

The national currency, the Moldovan leu (plural: lei), was introduced in November 1993. Each leu is made up of one hundred bani (singular is ban). Transnistria uses the Transnistrian ruble instead, even though it is not honored by Moldova or any other nation.

Gross domestic product (GDP) is a measure of a country's total production. The number reflects the total value of goods and services produced over one year. Economists use it to determine whether a country's economy is growing or contracting. Growth is good, while a falling GDP means trouble. Dividing the GDP by the number of people in the country determines the GDP per capita (per person). This number provides an indication of a country's average standard of living—the higher the better.

In 2017, the GDP per capita in Moldova was approximately $6,700. That figure is considered quite low, and it ranked Moldova at 162nd out of 228 countries listed by the CIA World Factbook. (For comparison, the United States that year was number 19, with a GDP per capita of $59,500; Russia was number 74 with $27,900; and Romania was number 83 with $24,600.)

In addition, the Moldovan labor force is mismatched to the needs of the labor market. Lacking the necessary skills to meet today's highly specialized workforce needs at home, many Moldovans find it hard to get a job. Many go abroad for lower-level work. The money they send home, called remittances, adds a large chunk to Moldova's economy. In recent years, some one million Moldovans working in Europe, Israel, Russia, and other countries sent home annual remittances of about $1.2 billion—almost 15 percent of Moldova's entire gross domestic product (GDP).

Many people just leave the country for good. That, combined with a falling birthrate, has led to a constantly shrinking population in recent years—another economic disadvantage.

Moldova enjoys a favorable climate and good farmland, but has no significant mineral deposits. As a result, the economy relies heavily on agriculture. The country has to import energy sources such as petroleum, coal, and natural gas from Russia. This heavy energy dependence gives Russia a great deal of power over Moldova, literally and figuratively, which it manipulates according to its own interests. Moldova's economy is further hampered by its reputation for corruption and a lack of transparency in business and government operations.

POVERTY LINE

In 2015, about 9.6 percent of Moldovans were living below the poverty line. This represents great improvement for Moldova, compared to its standing in prior years. In 2001, for example, some 54.6 percent of its people were living in poverty, according to the World Bank.

People in Chisinau walk past a homeless man.

However, it's difficult to compare this statistic across different countries because definitions of poverty vary considerably among nations. Wealthier nations, for example, tend to use a more generous poverty line than poorer countries do. For instance, France—a much wealthier nation than Moldova—reported 14.2 percent of the population living below the poverty line that same year of 2015. Using more standardized criteria, though, such as GDP per capita, Moldova remains one of the poorest countries in Europe, despite its improvement.

MARKET ECONOMY

Moldova's economy is limited by its small size and landlocked location. Another limiting factor is that, except for very small gas and oil reserves, the country is totally dependent on energy imports, mainly from Russia. Industry provides jobs for less than 12 percent of the labor force, while agriculture employs around 32.3 percent.

Like many of the other former Soviet republics, Moldova experienced a sharp downturn in its economy after the breakup of the Soviet Union in 1991. Since its economy was highly dependent on Russia for energy and raw materials, the breakdown in trade and energy shortages following the collapse of the Soviet Union had a serious effect, exacerbated at times by drought and civil conflict. Energy shortages also contributed to sharp production declines. After the Russian ruble devaluation of 1998, Moldova's economy underwent a prolonged recession.

Moldova has since made significant progress in economic reform, after it started to emerge from the recession in 2000. These reforms helped maintain Moldova's macroeconomic and financial stability under very difficult circumstances. It introduced its own currency, the leu, to replace the Russian ruble and transformed its economic system to a market economy—that is, a capitalistic system in which there is free competition between private businesses, and prices are determined by the forces of supply and demand. It liberalized prices for most of its commodities, backed land privatization, removed export controls, and freed interest rates. As a result, its GDP grew to an all-time high in 2017 of $8.13 billion, as compared to a record low of $1.17 billion in 1999.

AGRICULTURE

Moldova's proximity to the Black Sea gives it a mild and sunny climate, making it ideal for agriculture, which accounts for 17.7 percent of the country's GDP. Crops such as berries, wine, tobacco, vegetables, sugar beets, potatoes, and sunflowers have traditionally accounted for the biggest share of agricultural

A field of sunflowers outside Chisinau makes for a cheerful sight.

Moldova's economy is small enough that a giant trade partner can wreak havoc just by refusing its goods. Russia has been using this approach to manipulate Moldova for several years.

In 2005, strained political relations between the two countries led Russia to ban Moldovan agricultural products. In 2006, Russia banned imports of Moldovan wines. This slowed down the small country's economy greatly, during a period when other economic forces were compounding the situation. In 2007, a twofold increase in gas prices and a severe drought resulted in hundreds of millions of dollars in agricultural-sector losses and prompted widespread concerns about food availability.

Russia's wine ban was particularly painful for Moldova because, prior to the ban, Moldovan wines accounted for almost one-third of the country's exports, and 80 percent of wine exports went to Russia. Although Russian president Vladimir Putin announced an end to the wine ban in November 2006, actual resumption of wine exports came a year later. The ban provided an important lesson for Moldova, however. Some Moldovan wineries have taken advantage of current European trade agreements as incentive for further market diversification and have been successful in finding new, alternative markets for their products. Russia was not pleased. In 2013, it once again imposed a ban on Moldovan wines.

And that was not the end. In 2014, Russia banned imports of apples, plums, peaches, and canned fruit from Moldova. This ban caused great harm to Moldova's fruit growers (above right). After all, in 2013, Russia bought 43 percent ($988 million) of all of Moldova's agricultural exports. Many Moldovan farmers blamed their own government for their losses. Analysts suggested that Russia's purpose in embargoing the fruit was an attempt to turn Moldovan voters against the pro-Western/pro-EU factions in their government in the upcoming elections.

In 2017, Russia banned some 20 tons (18 metric tons) of Moldovan plums after the Moldovan government banned a Russian official from entering the country. This in turn was a protest against Russia's annexation of Ukraine's Crimean Peninsula—a land grab that Russia could easily repeat with Transnistria.

production. The fertile soil also supports wheat, corn, barley, and soybeans. Its orchards produce significant amounts of fruit, including plums, peaches, apricots, and cherries.

Moldova also produces walnuts, sugar, vegetable oils, meat, and dairy products. Moldova's best-known wines come from its extensive and well-developed vineyards concentrated in the central and southern regions. In addition to world-class wine, Moldova produces liqueurs, brandies, and champagnes.

Deep purple grapes ripen on the vine in a wine-producing region of Moldova.

INDUSTRY

Food processing (including sugar and vegetable oils) is the largest domestic industry in Moldova, followed by manufacturing—agricultural machinery, foundry equipment, refrigerators, freezers, and washing machines, as well as hosiery, footwear, and textiles. In the processed fruit and vegetable sector, field tomatoes and apples account for a large portion of all output, which also includes canned goods, dehydrated fruits, purees for baby food, jams and preserves, and some specialty products.

Sugar beets are an important crop for Moldova, the country's third-largest crop after wheat and corn. The beets are grown throughout the country and provide raw material for a substantial sugar-refining industry. In 2018, Moldova produced about 775,000 tons (703,000 metric tons) of sugar beets, a decline from the larger crops of the 1990s, when between 1 and 2 million-plus tons a year was more typical.

Wine represents a major component of Moldova's economy. The republic is known for its quality wines and is an important regional producer of grapes and grape products, with some 140 wineries. Moldova's wine industry was hurt by Russia's 2006 ban on imports of wine, and the need to diversify its markets became apparent. In 2004, some 90 percent of Moldovan wine exports were sold to CIS countries (particularly Russia, Kazakhstan, Ukraine, and Belurus).

By 2018, however, that figure decreased to 31 percent, and more markets were found in the West—Poland, Romania, Czechia, and Slovakia.

Factories in Moldova produce electronic equipment, machinery, automation and telecommunications equipment, television sets, electric engines, pumps, tractors and other agricultural machinery, refrigerators, and other appliances. The light industry sector manufactures carpets, textiles, garments, and footwear. New industries such as scrap-metal processing, chemicals, and medical equipment have emerged since independence. In addition, the construction materials industry is expanding through exports of cement, gypsum, and ceramics, and through investment in civil engineering.

Many Moldovans still make wine the old-fashioned way. This squeezer presses the juice out of the fruit.

ENERGY

Among the most pressing concerns facing Moldova's economy is its lack of energy resources. The country has few oil reserves and no refineries. It depends almost entirely on Russia, Ukraine, and Romania for oil, coal, and natural gas.

A hydroelectric plant on the Dniester River in Dubăsari.

About 12 percent of Moldova's electric energy is produced by the hydropower plants located on the Dniester and Prut Rivers, but these are insufficient for the densely populated country. Some 86 percent of its electricity is produced using fossil fuels. Consumption of electricity in 2016 was 4.4 billion kilowatts.

In a bid to expand its energy resources and decrease its dependence on imports, Moldova is seeking alternative sources and is working to develop its renewable energy supplies, such as solar power, wind, and geothermal. A mere 2 percent of its electricity comes from such sources. The country also has a national energy-conservation program.

Just as Russia has tried to manipulate Moldova by banning Moldovan agricultural imports, it has also cut off energy supplies for the same purpose. In 2006, Russian energy company Gazprom temporarily cut off natural-gas supplies to Ukraine and Moldova and subsequently doubled the price of gas to Moldova. A similar occurrence took place in 2009. Some of Moldova's vulnerability is linked to Russia's similar treatment of Ukraine, as the pipeline linking Moldova and Russia flows through Ukraine.

In order to lessen its energy dependence on Russia, Moldova has sought out other alternatives. In 2015, Moldova and Romania opened the Ungheni-Iasi natural gas interconnector project. The 26.7-mile (43 km) pipeline between Moldova and Romania allows for both the import and export of natural gas. The pipeline is due to be expanded to Chisinau, and Moldova also hopes to connect with the European power grid by 2022.

INFRASTRUCTURE

The infrastucture of Moldova is well developed. Its road network is more than 10,439 miles (16,800 km) long, of which slightly more than 1,864 miles (3,000 km) are important highways, and the rest are local roads.

As an agricultural country, Moldova depends on a reliable transportation network to ensure the efficient domestic movement of produce and the export of agricultural goods. Railroads transport 95 percent of exports. The rail system

Highways intersect in Chisinau, as seen in this aerial view.

The Moldovan flag waves in the breeze on a ferry as it crosses the Dniester River.

extends for 803 miles (1,292 km) and carries a large amount of important exports and imports.

Air transportation is provided by private carriers and a state company, Air Moldova. Chisinau International Airport is the country's main commercial airport. It serves about 2,830,000 passengers each year.

The Dniester and Prut Rivers are used for ferrying tourists and local cargo. However, parts of the Dniester are fully under the control of the Transnistrian authorities. The construction of a port and a fuel terminal is scheduled at the meeting point of the Prut and the Danube to serve tankers and other ships. Moldova also has one small oil terminal on the Danube at Cahul which can accommodate small seagoing vessels. The harbor opened in 2006 and occupies the entire Moldovan stretch of the river, a mere 1,969 feet (600 m).

PUBLIC TRANSPORTATION

Moldova's well-developed public transportation network is largely credited to the extensive amount of highways and municipal, agricultural, and forestry roads. Local transport in Moldova includes trams, buses, and the old-fashioned trolleybuses. However, traveling by road or rail are the two most common modes of transportation for local Moldovans.

Trolleybuses provide transportation in the wintertime in Chisinau.

Between nations, too, Moldova is also well served by buses connecting Chisinau with Kiev, Bucharest, and other key cities in Romania and Ukraine. A lot of these border crossings may take as long as ten hours, but the buses provide a cheap means of transport for many rural dwellers who work in the cities.

INTERNET LINKS

https://www.heritage.org/index/country/moldova
The Index of Economic Freedom examines the country's economic climate.

https://www.theguardian.com/world/2014/aug/15/ moldova-fights-back-russia-food-bans
This article provides information on Russian bans on Moldovan agricultural products.

http://www.3dcftas.eu/publications/other/expanding-iasi -ungheni-pipeline-chisinau-challenges-and-opportunities
This article explains the proposed Romania—Moldova natural gas pipeline, including concerns about its feasibility and effectiveness.

ENVIRONMENT

A wind turbine spins in a green field in Gordinestii Noi, a village in Edinet in the north of Moldova.

MOLDOVA IS A RELATIVELY FLAT country, with one-third of its land covered by fertile plains and terraces. Colorful orchards, fields of grain, and sunflowers dot the countryside. It is a country blessed with rich soils and a high percentage of arable land. Its terrain is further endowed with minerals and sedimetnary rocks, including sand, gravel, gypsum, and limestone.

However, economic development and agricultural pollution have led to a massive reduction in Moldova's biodiversity, particularly its steppe and wetland habitats. Heavy use of agricultural chemicals, particularly during the Soviet years, along with poor farming methods and overexploitation have resulted in soil degradation and contaminated groundwater. Soil erosion washes away millions of tons of fertile soil annually. It also leads to landslides, which are a natural hazard in Moldova.

5

The Orhei National Park, established in 2013, is Moldova's only national park, though there are five scientific nature reserves. The Orhei park, covering 83,520 acres (33,800 hectares), was established to preserve biodiversity, stop the degradation of forestry ecosystems, restore sustainable management of forests and pastures, preserve cultural and architectural-historical heritage, and promote environmentally friendly farming and ecotourism.

An aerial view shows Moldova's relatively flat rural areas.

Air, water, and industrial pollution are widespread and are the attributed cause of Moldova's high rates of abnormal births and infant mortalities. In many parts of the country, levels of nitrate, chloride, iron, and fecal bacteria are well above the levels considered safe by the World Health Organization (WHO).

LAND

The soils of Moldova are varied and highly fertile, with chernozem—rich black soils—covering 75 percent of the republic. Moldova's agricultural productivity is due largely to its rich soils. The best chernozem, which feeds the growth of grain, tobacco, and sugar beets, is found in the north and in low-lying parts of the central and Dniester uplands, as well as in the left-bank regions. Excessive use of chemical fertilizers, pesticides, and herbicides during the Soviet period, however, resulted in extensive contamination of Moldova's soil and groundwater. For more than fifty years, Moldova was part of the Soviet

Union, with an economy based on agriculture and food processing. During this time, 75 percent of the land was devoted to agriculture. Small farms were converted into large agricultural enterprises and state farms, and they were saturated with chemicals to increase production.

Unsustainable use of land and heavy machinery resulted in severe degradation of the environment. Large cattle, pig, and poultry farms that lacked proper waste management facilities were established near major rivers. The discharge of untreated animal waste and manure was until recently a major pollutant of Moldova's groundwater and drinking water supply.

FORESTS

Forests in Moldova cover about 11 percent of the country's territory, or 951,356 acres (385,000 ha). Northern and central Moldova is a forest zone, while a steppe belt encompasses the south. Moldova's steppes were originally grass covered, but now most of them are cultivated. The most common trees are hornbeam and oak, followed by linden, maple, wild pear, and wild cherry.

A terraced green hillside backs up to a forest in the Codri region.

Beech forests are commonly found around the Ikel and Bac Rivers. The republic has five scientific reserves, two of which are forest reserves, while three are forest-aquatic reserves. Totaling an area of 47,884 acres (19,378 ha), the reserves protect natural areas of bird migration, old beech and oak forests, and major waterways. Moldova's oldest and most popular reserve is the Codri Reserve. It is home to some 924 plant species, 138 bird species, and 45 species of mammals. In 2013, Moldova established a new national park in the Orhei region.

Moldova's forest biodiversity is rich. However, poor forest management led to a reduction in forest quality and a decrease of biodiversity in certain areas. Very little research and training is carried out in the areas of biodiversity protection and conservation, the development and management of natural areas, and the protection of vulnerable and endangered species of animals and plants. Like many other former Soviet republics, Moldova lacks the financial resources and institutional capacity to implement the provisions of the Convention on Biological Diversity, to which Moldova is a signatory.

Other threats to forest biodiversity are deforestation, unauthorized grazing, and pollution due to municipal waste and unregulated tourism. Extensive deforestation has resulted in soil erosion, wind damage, a drop in the groundwater table, flooding, and loss of fauna. Well aware of the severity of problems caused by such a great loss of woodlands, environmentalists and scientists have lobbied for increased afforestation plans. As a result, large-scale reforestation projects were begun in the early 1990s. The projects were at first met with resistance from farmers who have been concerned that their agricultural and grazing lands would be converted into less profitable forests.

POLLUTION

SOIL POLLUTION   During the five decades of Soviet leadership, Moldova's agricultural land was heavily worked to produce cheap goods for the Soviet Union. Creation of new agricultural lands, careless cultivation, and the discharge of manure and other types of untreated animal waste all led to soil degradation.

The greatest pollution comes from excessive fertilization. The use of chemical fertilizers per acre was increased from year to year. By 1990, 25 percent of the food produced was polluted with nitrates. The Agricultural Pollution Control Project (APCP), a project of the World Bank, worked to educate farmers on sustainable practices in crop and livestock production in order to reduce this dependence on chemicals.

Other components of the APCP project included monitoring water and soil quality, restoring wetlands, and planting forest vegetation. In addition, the project scope included raising public awareness, and strengthening national legislation pertaining to agricultural pollution control.

A burning pile of garbage causes air pollution in the western city of Leova.

WATER POLLUTION   Almost 28 percent of the total population depends on surface water in Moldova, while the rest of the population consumes underground water. Almost 8 percent of the water comes from aquifers, and only half of the water meets drinking standards. Many of the rural wells are either drying up or contaminated with minerals and bacteria. Most of the river valleys and lake areas are in use for agricultural production, and Moldova has no system to remove chemicals and salt from the polluted water.

Water discharge is also a problem. Some 70 percent of households in Moldova are not connected to sewers or wastewater treatment facilities. This situation is a major source of organic and microbial pollution in the waterways and soils.

AIR POLLUTION   Under the Soviets, pollution controls were not installed, and emissions from factories in neighboring republics drifted over Moldova. Today polluted air is mostly found in Balti, Rabnita, Chisinau, and Tiraspol, and three-quarters of it is caused by cars—many of which are old cars. Large numbers of used cars are imported from Europe, but there are still quite a few old Soviet cars on the road. These old vehicles have no emissions controls and pour untreated pollutants into the air.

WATER SUPPLY

Moldova has a well-developed network of rivers and streams, all draining south to the Black Sea. The marshy lower reaches of Moldova's rivers provide respite for wild geese, migratory ducks, and herons, whereas white-tailed sea eagles are found in the floodplain forests. Underground water, extensively used for the republic's water supply, includes some 2,200 natural springs.

The Dniester River supplies 56 percent of the Moldova's needs and the Prut River provides about 16 percent. But in spite of the country's 3,621 water courses, occasional water shortages occur due to low precipitation and high evaporation rates. These shortages lead to crop failure, and rivers and wells drying up. To add to the problem, the Prut and Dniester are contaminated by intensive agricultural production and industrial wastes.

Although Moldova has more than three thousand rivers and streams, only about one-tenth of them exceed 6.2 miles (10 km) in length, and even fewer exceed 62 miles (100 km). Many of the small, shallow streams dry up during the summer. Moldova does not have any large lakes, and all of its larger rivers originate outside its borders.

Since water resources are of particular importance to Moldova, water pollution is viewed as a significant threat. The republic has difficulties securing adequate supplies of potable water and reducing the pollution levels in existing supplies. Only 8 percent of Moldova's water comes from aquifers, and only 50 percent of this meets drinking standards.

WATER SERVICES

Moldova's municipal water sector is still suffering from years of neglect and underinvestment. Raw water resources are polluted, and water treatment plants are no longer able to meet quality standards. Many of the smaller towns get their water supply from groundwater sources that do not meet hygiene standards. These towns typically experience daily power cuts, resulting in a lack of water pressure in the network and a reduction in water quality.

As for wastewater treatment, most such plants in Moldova were designed for both mechanical and biological treatment. However, as a result of inadequate maintenance, regular power cuts, low water pressure in the network, and limited finances, most wastewater treatment plants operate on mechanical treatment only.

STATE ACCOUNTABILITY

The Republic of Moldova has two tiers of local government: municipal (villages and towns) and *judets* (zhu-DETS), or counties. The responsibility of regulating environmental standards lies with the environmental inspectors at the judets level. The provision of services, such as municipal solid waste management, water supply, and wastewater collection and treatment, is the responsibility of the municipalities.

Many of Moldova's local officials, however, have very limited knowledge of the country's environmental issues. They are faced with an astonishing range of environmental and social problems at a time when there is strong pressure for change. They must also come to terms with tougher environmental laws influenced by the EU, such as Moldova's Framework Directive on Water.

What's more, Moldova's environmental issues are becoming more and more acute and expensive to solve. Climate change is causing an increase in drought, and for a heavily agricultural country like Moldova, that poses a huge problem.

INTERNET LINKS

http://green.gov.md/index.php?l=en
Sustainable Green Development of Moldova focuses on current environmental issues in Moldova.

http://www.md.undp.org/content/moldova/en/home/ climate-change-environment-energy.html
This UN Development Programme site focuses on environmental topics relevant to Moldova.

MOLDOVANS

A Moldovan dancer poses for a photo at a folk dance competition in 2018.

6

MOLDOVA HAS A POPULATION density of 316 persons per square mile (122 per sq km). Most of its population lives in the northern and central parts of the country. During the Soviet period, Moldova had the highest population density among the Soviet republics.

POPULATION TRENDS

The multiethnic population of Moldova reflects the complexity of its history. Of its 3.4 million people—excluding the breakaway region of Transnistria; 3.9 million including it—some 75.1 percent are Moldovan. Of the remaining population, 7 percent are Romanian; 6.6 percent are Ukrainian; 4.6 percent are Gagauz; 4.1 percent are Russians, and 1.9 percent are Bulgarian (figures are from 2014). Smaller ethnic minorities such as the Gagauz and Bulgarians reside in rural enclaves in the south. These ethnic communities have their own degree of regional autonomy.

The Gagauz people are a Turkic people (which is not the same thing as Turkish people, or people from Turkey, though there is a slight connection). This ethnic/linguistic group of peoples speak related languages and share certain cultural traits, common ancestry, and historical backgrounds. They are found primarily in populations throughout Central and North Asia, and to a much lesser extent, in some parts of Eastern Europe. Nomadic tribes from Mongolia and Central Asia might have brought some of these peoples to Eastern Europe. Or the Turkic population might have arrived with the Hun invasions of the West in the fourth and fifth centuries CE. However it was that they first came to the region, their descendants remain today. The Gagauz people of Moldova are but one of many Turkic peoples.

WHERE PEOPLE LIVE

Moldovans reside in 65 cities and towns, and in more than 1,575 villages. Only 42.6 percent live in cities, a figure that has been dropping at a rate of 0.07 percent per year from 2015 to 2020. Most city dwellers live in Chisinau, Balti, Tiraspol, and Tighina, with some 510,000 living in Chisinau in 2018.

THE QUESTION OF IDENTITY

Moldova joins two regions, Bessarabia and Transnistria, into one country. Bessarabia consists predominantly of ethnic Romanians and constitutes

the western half of the country. Transnistria is Slavic, and its people are ethnic Ukrainians and Russians. Viewed as a whole, Moldova has a majority population of ethnic Romanians. Despite Soviet efforts to Russianize them, most ethnic Romanians maintained their identity and looked to Romania as the source of their culture. When the Soviet Union crumbled, Moldova asserted its independence, although people were far from unanimous on the issue. The nationalists eventually succeeded. Moldova sought to distance itself from Russia. But the Transnistrians wanted no part of independent Moldova, its ethnic-Romanian nationalists, or reunification with Romania, where they would be a small minority instead of a powerful political force.

While the language and culture of the majority is largely Romanian, the Soviet period saw a dominance of the Russian language in economics, politics, education, and any attempts at modernization. In addition, Russian influence

Thousands of people gather on March 25, 2018, in the Great National Assembly Square in Chisinau to mark the hundred-year anniversary of the union of Bessarabia with Romania.

brought a large influx of Ukrainians and Russians to Moldova, particularly to its urban centers. Their descendants have now been in Moldova for several generations and consider it home.

Soviet leader Joseph Stalin further strengthened his hold by making Russian the official language and favoring ethnic Russians for government positions. He was able to exert power over Moldovans by reducing their population majority, concentrating the industrial centers in Russian-speaking Ukrainian-dominated areas, and increasing their dependence on such areas for industrial produce. As a result, Moldovan urbanites in general, despite their ethnic backgrounds, adopted the Russian language and national identity to some degree. The rural-urban divide was also obvious, with Russian spoken widely in cities and national languages spoken in rural areas.

Complicating this struggle of identities have been regional conflicts involving minority groups such as ethnic Russians and Gagauz fighting for more autonomy and independence. The military conflict between Transnistria and

The Stalinist House of Soviets building in Tiraspol, Transnistria, features a bust of Vladimir Lenin at the entrance.

Moldova in 1992 is an example of this. Transnistria and Moldova went to war when the Soviet empire was dissolved and Transnistria tried to claim independence from Moldova. The dispute was said to be driven by culture, religion, and ethnic nationalism. The region successfully defeated Moldovan forces, with the help of Russia. Today, the Russian-speaking population of Transnistria continues to maintain an independent Soviet quality, although the territory is unrecognized as independent. While a cease-fire has been maintained ever since, the Council of Europe recognizes Transnistria as a "frozen conflict" region.

A group of young women enjoy chatting at a café in Chisinau.

MOLDOVAN CHARACTER

Moldovans have managed to maintain strong family ties, traditions, a rich culture, and a love of beauty and the arts. Moldovans are generally friendly and kind. This is especially true in the villages, where the communal bond is close-knit. Moldovans love to socialize and make people feel comfortable. Friends will stop by each other's homes without prior notice because they know they will be welcome. People are also not aggressive or competitive by nature. Moldovans generally do not enter into fighting with their own people. Any hostility or violence toward others is usually caused by the potent force of nationalism and by extreme differences of political opinion.

LOCAL CUSTOMS

Moldovan men greet each other with a handshake. When a man sees a male acquaintance in a group and greets him with a handshake, it would be impolite not to shake the hands of all the other males in the group as well. Moldovan women do not shake hands, however. In either a business or a social setting, a nod of the head is acceptable when greeting a woman.

In Moldova, shoes that are worn outdoors are removed when entering a home or an apartment. Moldovans normally change into slippers indoors. A host would be extremely offended if guests were to wear their shoes in his home.

TRADITIONAL DRESS

Moldovans wear the same everyday clothing as most people in the rest of Europe and the West. Traditional costumes are reserved for special occasions such as folk festivals.

A distinctive feature of the Moldovan national dress is the embroidery on both men's and women's clothes. The rich colors of red, black, and gold embroidery complement each other and contrast with a white background. A woman's blouse is loose-fitting with three-quarter or full-length sleeves, worn with a white skirt. Over the skirt, a dark-colored apron with woven geometric patterns is tied at the waist with a sash. Regional differences are reflected in the colors and patterns of embroidery used. Cotton and silk, or

On Independence Day, August 27, holiday concert performers dress in traditional costumes.

wool for the winter, are the preferred fabrics. These clothes are traditionally spun and sewn by women. Women wear colored scarves with a white border of lace on their heads and tied under at the nape. Strings of beads around the neck and long dangling pearl earrings complete the outfit.

The men's national dress is a long-sleeve white shirt, worn with narrow trousers that are secured at the waist with a sash or a leather belt. An embroidered sleeveless vest is worn over the shirt. Headgear for men is a tall hat made of lambskin, felt, or even straw for the summer. Traditional footwear is the moccasin, a type of soft leather slipper, or boots.

INTERNET LINKS

https://www.huffingtonpost.com/2014/08/14/moldova-life -photos_n_5668888.html
A photo essay portrays poor Moldovan children whose parents left the country to look for work.

https://www.moldova.org/en/2014-census-results-finally -published-moldovas-population-29-million-people
The results of Moldova's 2014 census are reported on this site. (Note: The Moldovan census figures differ slightly from the demographic statistics used in this book, which are from the *CIA World Factbook*, based on estimates made by the US Bureau of the Census.)

https://www.wired.com/2016/03/meet-people-transnistria-stucka -time-soviet-country-doesnt-exist
This article highlights the strange circumstance of living in an unofficial country.

http://www.worldharmonyrun.org/moldova/news/2012.html
This website of an international fun run that ran through Moldova in 2012 offers a wealth of good photos of Moldovan people throughout the country, many in traditional dress.

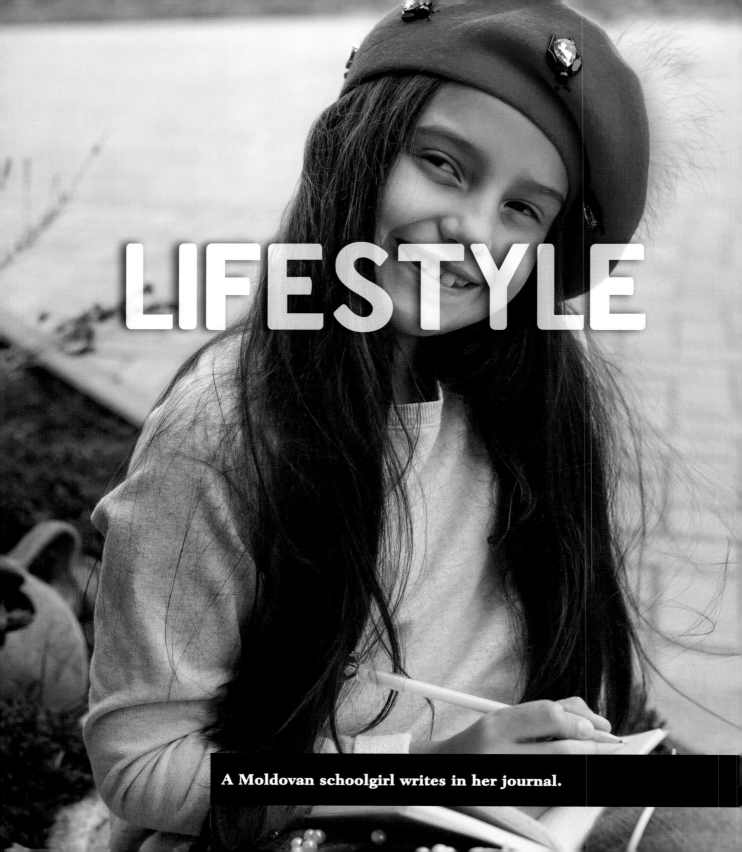

LIFESTYLE

A Moldovan schoolgirl writes in her journal.

FOR MOST MOLDOVANS, LIFE revolves around the love of family, care of the land, development as a nation, and ties with the larger European society. Chisinau offers modern European city living, whereas the countryside offers rustic charm from the past. Older people, who lived through the Soviet years and the hard economic times that followed independence, hope that the worst is behind them. For young people, living in Europe's poorest country can mean a lack of opportunity that prompts many to look for work in other countries.

FAMILY AND KINSHIP

It is not unusual to find three generations of a family living in the same house in Moldova. Although this can mainly be attributed to the difficulty of finding housing, it is also a reflection of Moldovan family values. The family is very important to Moldovans, and the average urban family has two or three children. Rural families may have more children. Children generally grow up close to their grandparents, who teach them songs and

7

In 2016, Moldova spent 6.7 percent of its GDP on public education. This rate was the 21st highest of 180 countries. Cross-country comparisons, however, can be misleading. A high proportion of government spending doesn't necessarily equal higher academic achievement, especially if a country's GDP is low to begin with. However, a higher rate can sometimes lead to academic improvement.

An elderly couple wait on the porch of their country home for a visit from their family.

fairy tales. Girls are expected to help their mothers from an early age and to take care of younger siblings.

From the time they are young children, Moldovans are taught to respect and care for older people. There are few nursing homes for the elderly and the disabled, as families are expected to take care of their own. Within a family, if there are older members, the rest would try their best to provide for them. Placing a family member in an aged-care institution is definitely a last resort. Relatives support one other in performing agricultural and other tasks as well as in ceremonial obligations.

The godparenthood system regulates mutual obligations between the parties. Godparents are responsible for the children they sponsor at baptism, especially marriage and the building of a house. Godparenthood is inherited through the generations; however, it is also common for this role to be negotiated independently of previous ties.

SOCIAL CUSTOMS

Moldovans greatly enjoy visiting friends and relatives. Most socializing takes place in the home. On special occasions, guests are treated to feasts. Otherwise, people sit in the kitchen or the living room and chat for hours. Hosts generally provide guests with coffee, tea, wine, or cognac. Vodka is popular among the Russian minority. Guests often bring small gifts, and hosts, especially in rural areas, usually reciprocate with a small gift such as a cake "for the next morning" or wine. It is proper to drink at least a symbolic amount of wine during a meal or in a ritual context to honor the host and toast the health of the people present. Occasionally in villages, toasting with the left hand may not be regarded as proper.

Food is almost always prepared by the women in the family; it is considered embarrassing for a man to admit he cooks. When guests are present, the hosts offer additional helpings; it is polite to decline two or three times before accepting. Leaving food on the plate may be considered a sign that a guest has not enjoyed the meal. It is also improper to blow one's nose at the table. Smoking in homes is an uncommon practice; both hosts and guests usually go outside or onto the balcony to smoke. In villages, it is highly improper for women to smoke in public.

Interaction differs in urban and rural areas. In the villages, people are friendly and greet passersby without prior acquaintance; in the cities, there is a greater anonymity, although people interact with strangers in certain situations—for example, on public transportation. Foreign visitors are considered honored guests and are treated with great respect and hospitality. Moldovans are usually very keen to hear what foreigners think of their country. Visitors, in turn, are struck by the warmth of the Moldovan people.

FOOD CUSTOMS

Orthodox Christian baptisms, funerals, and weddings are accompanied by large gatherings where several meat and vegetable dishes, desserts, and cakes, as

A family get-together is an occasion for a feast of favorite Moldovan specialities.

well as wine, are served. Homemade vodka and brandy are also offered. At Easter, a special bread, *pasca* (pas-KUH), is baked in every household, and eggs are painted in various colors. Families go to the cemetery to commemorate their dead kin; they eat food at the graves, drink wine, and share their meals with each other as they remember the dead.

LIFE EVENTS

To Moldovans, baptisms, weddings, and funerals are the most important life-cycle rituals and are combined with church attendance and social gatherings. Orthodox Christians typically marry in a church ceremony, which is followed by a party with dancing and plenty to eat and drink. In the rural areas, any stranger who enters the village on the day of the marriage is invited to join in the festivities and is welcomed as part of the family. Local musicians play lively music, and tables are set up in a central communal area for the feast. Giving money rather than presents is a traditional custom, and a plate is passed around to collect money for the couple.

Friends and family jump for joy beside a newlywed couple in November 2016. Behind them, a stretch limousine awaits in Cathedral Park in Chisinau.

Newlyweds usually live together with the groom's parents until they can build a house in the village or rent an apartment in town. In the villages, there is a general rule of ultimogeniture—the youngest son and his family live with the parents, and he inherits the contents of the household.

Another happy occasion Moldovans celebrate is the birth of a child. If the infant's parents are Orthodox Christians, the child is christened in the church, and guests are invited to the parents' house for refreshments. Babies are taken care of by their mothers and grandmothers. In villages, babies are wrapped in blankets during the very early months, and cloth diapers are used.

Funerals are solemn events, and the deceased are treated with utmost respect. Ideally the body is laid in an open casket and watched over for three days. Relatives and friends come to the house to pay their respects to the family. Food and drink, prepared by the family, are served to the mourners.

A baby is baptized according to Orthodox tradition in a church in Chisinau.

A porridge of cooked wheat and sugar called *coliva* (kol-ly-va) is prepared and offered to guests. The thick mixture, which can be molded into cakes, resembles soil, or earth. It is often decorated with crosses or other religious symbols, and candles. Usually the burial is within three days of death.

Platters of *coliva* are decorated with religious symbols for a somber occasion.

RECREATION

In their spare time, Moldovans visit friends, go to the movies, or read. Football (soccer), badminton, basketball, volleyball, swimming, and ice skating are popular sports among teenagers and young adults. Public facilities are available, but most are in need of repair. Many Moldovans love music and the arts, and they particularly enjoy attending concerts and festivals. Folk music is especially popular at national festivals.

No doubt because of the number of young people who flock to the capital for work and study, Chisinau has a thriving nightlife, boasting a multitude of clubs with cutting-edge decor and design. Outside of the capital, however, nightlife is very limited.

RITUALS

The Orthodox calendar dictates rituals and celebrations throughout the year, such as Christmas, Easter, and several saints' days. Some of the customary rules include fasting or avoiding meat and meat fat as well as restrictions on washing, bathing, and working at particular times. Easter is celebrated in church and by visiting the graves of kin. Candles are an inseparable part of rituals for Moldovans; people buy candles when they enter the church and light them in front of the icons or during rituals.

EDUCATION

Moldova has an adult literacy rate of 99.4 percent. Nevertheless, the Moldovan education system was struggling in the early part of the twenty-first century.

In 2009, Moldovan students were found to be scoring below average across all areas of study, according to the Programme for International Student Assessment (PISA), an initiative administered by the Organisation for Economic Co-operation and Development (OECD).

By 2015, however, academic performance was improving. This came in the wake of increased funding of education and accountability requirements implemented by the Moldovan government in 2013. However, there were significant gaps in achievement between urban and rural communities, with rural students lagging behind.

Education is compulsory for children ages seven to sixteen. Schooling is broken into three levels, not including early childhood education or higher education.

High school students in Drochia, Moldova, file down the stairs past a world map.

Primary school is grades one through four. Secondary education is split into two tiers, lower and upper. Lower secondary, grades five to nine, is called *gymnasium*. Gymnasium graduates must pass an entrance exam to qualify for the upper secondary level, called *lyceum*. Those who don't get into lyceum can attend general or vocational schools through grade twelve but will not be able to go on to university. Lyceum includes grades ten through twelve. Students who wish to continue on to college or university must pass the national baccalaureate exam.

According to a 2016 World Bank report, enrollment in Moldova's upper secondary level was only 54 percent in the 2014—2015 school year. Students in lower-income families were more likely to attend vocational studies rather than higher-level academics.

Under the Soviet system, most schools were taught in the Russian language. Moldovans who were educated in Russian-speaking schools still have difficulty expressing themselves in Moldovan in instances other than daily encounters. Moldovans who were born after 1980 tend to speak less and less Russian, a trend that could lead to growing problems of interethnic communication. Except for in the autonomous regions of Transnistria and Gagauzia, the language of instruction in Moldovan schools is Romanian.

In the 2017—2018 school year, Moldova had 1,358 educational institutions, including 1,243 primary and secondary general education institutions, 86 technical schools, and 29 institutions of higher education. The student population has been declining across all levels, reflecting the country's general population decline in recent years.

GENDER ROLES

Women in both the urban and rural areas carry the burden of domestic duties and childcare in addition to working outside the home. As a result of tradition and economic necessity, women often engage in domestic food-processing activities in the summer to provide home-canned food for the bleak winter months.

Although men seem to have more decision-making power in the public and private spheres, women generally act as the organizers of daily and ritual life.

They organize social gatherings, gift-giving practices, and the infrastructure of numerous official and semiofficial events.

Moldova has publicly committed to gender equality, at least in theory. But according to UN Women, a UN organization dedicated to gender equality and the empowerment of women, Moldovan women face discrimination and inequality in social, economic, and political life. Some of these practices include significant wage disparities, a disproportionate number of women in lower-paying occupations, and the unequal sharing of work and family responsibilities mentioned above. In addition, women looking to start businesses often face barriers getting access to bank loans and to state-funded development programs.

Violence against women is a deeply rooted social problem in Moldova. In 2011, the Moldova's National Bureau of Statistics found that 63 percent of women experienced psychological, physical, or sexual violence at the hands of their husband or partner. Rural, elderly, and separated or divorced women were found to be the most vulnerable to multiple types of violence.

INTERNET LINKS

http://eca.unwomen.org/en/where-we-are/moldova
This is the UN Women site for Moldova.

https://medium.com/this-is-moldova/the-life-of-a-moldovan -peasant-864ee5412291
This substantial slide show portrays typical rural life in Moldova.

https://www.unicef.org/moldova
The Unicef (United Nations International Children's Emergency Fund) site for Moldova provides up-to-date statistics and archived articles relating to children's health, education, and other lifestyle information.

RELIGION

The red and white Monastery of the Nativity of the Mother of God, also known as the Curchi Monastery, is considered one of the most beautiful churches in Moldova.

8

MORE THAN 90 PERCENT OF Moldovans are Eastern Orthodox Christians. They belong primarily to one of two denominations—the Moldovan Orthodox Church (under the Russian Orthodox Church) and the Bessarabian Orthodox Church (under the Romanian Orthodox Church). By far, the large majority of people belong to the Moldovan Church, which has 1,194 parishes. The Bessarabian Church in Moldova has 124 parishes. About 0.09 percent of the population belongs to the Old Rite Russian Orthodox Church (also called Old Believers).

The other religious denominations are Roman Catholic and other forms of Christianity. Non-Christian religious groups such as Jews, Muslims, Hindus, and Buddhists make up less than 1 percent each of the population—sometimes quite a lot less. Altogether, there are some 2,600 religious communities registered in the country.

During the Soviet period, the communist government strictly limited the activities and practices of all religions. Since the collapse of the Soviet Union, however, most religions have undergone a revival and have

Most of Moldova's monasteries were closed by Soviet authorities. They were used as hospitals, sanatoriums, or even storage facilities—and some were damaged and neglected. The only monastery to remain open during the Soviet era was the Japca Monastery, which housed a convent of nuns. Today, many of the monasteries have been reopened and restored.

worked toward regaining their former prominence. Citizens in independent Moldova today have much greater religious freedom than they did under the Soviet regime.

Nevertheless, the Moldovan Orthodox Church holds enormous power in the country. It is a very conservative church and is very publically opposed to homosexuality and alternative forms of gender identity and expression.

EASTERN ORTHODOX CHURCH

The Eastern Orthodox Church is a Christian branch that separated from the Roman Catholic Church in the eleventh century. The split between the two churches was related to the division of the Roman Empire into Eastern and Western halves, the Eastern center being the city of Constantinople (now known as Istanbul) and the Western center being Rome. Conflict over issues of doctrine led to an irreconcilable division, and the patriarch of Constantinople and the pope of Rome excommunicated each other. Following this divorce, the two branches went in quite distinct directions, largely due to the different cultures of the west and the east.

For Eastern Christianity, mysticism is extremely important, and the idea of grace and the redeeming power of God's love is paramount. Eastern Christianity is widely practiced in Greece, Eastern Europe, the Middle East, and North Africa. According to many authorities, one of the reasons the Eastern liturgy has made a stronger impact on the Christian Church than its Western counterpart in these regions is that it has always been viewed as a total experience, appealing simultaneously to the emotional, intellectual, and aesthetic aspects of humanity. Western Christianity, on the other hand, portrays God as ultimately a judge. Followers of Western Christianity believe that one's actions in life will influence whether one can go to heaven after death.

Since 1992, the Bessarabian Orthodox Church had been negotiating with the Chisinau government to grant it legal status, but each of its formal appeals was refused until 2002, when the government finally registered the church. Despite fierce opposition from the rival Moldovan Orthodox Church, the government finally bowed to pressure from the European Court of Human Rights (ECHR) and the Council of Europe Parliamentary Assembly, which had given the Moldovan government a deadline of July 31, 2002, to register the church.

RELIGION UNDER SOVIET RULE

The Soviet government strictly limited religious activity and ordered the destruction of Orthodox churches in an attempt to destroy religion. Clergies were punished and sometimes imprisoned for leading services, but most Orthodox believers continued to practice their religion in secret. By the beginning of World War II, the church structure was almost completely destroyed throughout the country. Many priests were driven away.

The catastrophic course of combat in the beginning of World War II forced Soviet leader Joseph Stalin to mobilize all national resources for defense, including the Orthodox Church, as the people's moral force. Without delay,

"Icon" comes from a Greek word meaning "image." In the Eastern Orthodox Church, icons are religious paintings of a very particular kind, executed in a flat, two-dimensional style. They are usually depictions of Jesus Christ, the Virgin Mary, the saints, or angels. Some are scenes from the Bible. Often gold leaf adorns the surfaces of these paintings, as gold represents the radiance of heaven. These images hang inside the churches and are treated with extraordinary reverence.

An icon is traditionally regarded as a kind of window between the earthly and the spiritual worlds. It is a window through which a divine personage—a saint, or Christ himself—looks into the human world. The image recorded in the icon is a sacred one because the heavenly spirit is miraculously imprinted in a two-dimensional way on the icon. The faithful venerate an icon not to worship the object itself but rather to worship the divine image that is glorified by the object.

The gold iconostasis, or wall of icons, displays the saints in the Capriana Monastery.

Icon painting flourishes in monasteries. According to custom, an icon artist is expected to be a person of high morals and Christian ideals who prepares for his work by fasting and praying. The iconography is not a creation of the artist's imagination or whim but follows a pattern and subject prescribed by church tradition. Sometimes icons have metal covers, called oklads, made to protect them from human handling in devotions, to enhance their beauty, or as memorials. The oklads often are made of silver or gilded silver, and the metal is cut out to reveal the painted faces, hands, and feet of the icon beneath. Some oklads are studded with precious gemstones, diamonds, and pearls.

In a church, small icons are set on portable, cloth-draped lecterns, and large ones hang on the walls. Beeswax candles burn nearby. The faithful kiss and touch the icons, and light incense in front of them as acts of devotion. Icons are blessed with holy water and carried in processions both inside and outside the church.

These acts of respect, handed down from ancient cultural traditions, still survive worldwide in the Orthodox Church. In Orthodox homes, icons are displayed in special places of honor. To the Orthodox Christian, an icon is a constant reminder of God's presence in church, at home, and in life.

A protester holds up a small personal icon at a political rally in Chisinau, asking for divine intervention.

churches were opened for services, and clerics were released from prisons. Even after the war, the church hierarchy was greatly expanded, although some members of the clergy were still occasionally arrested. This process can be described as a rapprochement between church and state. The church, however, remained under state control. A new and widespread persecution of the church was subsequently instituted under the leadership of Nikita Khrushchev and Leonid Brezhnev.

Then, beginning in the late 1980s under Mikhail Gorbachev, new political and social freedoms resulted in the lifting of the remaining restrictions. The collapse of the Soviet Union in 1991 led to complete religious freedom. Since then, churches have been restored and repaired in towns and villages.

CHURCH ARCHITECTURE

The highly decorated style of the Eastern Orthodox Church originated in the Byzantine era. This style of architecture and icon painting has since grown into an important Moldovan art. The physical splendor of the churches is

The "winter church" of the Capriana Monastery was built in 1903 in the Neo-Byzantine style.

emphasized, and a standard style—the cross inscribed in a rectangle and the dome supported on piers—became the accepted style for Orthodox churches. Over time, windows were narrowed, roofs became steeper, and flat-dome profiles assumed the rotund form, which eventually became the most notable feature of Orthodox church architecture.

After Constantinople fell to the Turks in 1453, Russia launched a large-scale church building program. Church architecture began to lose the special features associated with the Byzantine heritage, becoming more national in character and increasingly illustrating the taste and thought of the people. The most important change in Russian church design in the sixteenth century was the introduction of the tiered tower and the tent-shaped roof, first developed in wood by Russia's carpenters. The basic types and structural forms of the Russian multi-columned and tented churches were fully developed in the sixteenth century.

The Hancu Monastery in Bursuc, Moldova, was used as a sanitorium for people with tuberculosis during the Soviet years. In 1992, it was re-established as a convent, and reconstruction brought it back to its original beauty.

There are several extraordinary cave monasteries in Moldova. Centuries ago, monks lived lives of isolation and deprivation in the damp, cold rock cells. Today, some of the cave complexes have been restored and are open to tourists and religious pilgrims, though access can be very difficult.

One is the famous Rock Cave Church of the Annunciation, an underground monastery in the village of Saharna. This site is along the Dniester River, about 68 miles (110 km) north of Chisinau. Some sources say the old church was founded in 1495; others say its beginnings have been lost to history. Nearby is the Holy Trinity Monastery, an above-ground complex

The Holy Trinity chapel is perched high on a mountain cliff.

Stairs lead to a statue of Mary and the baby Jesus at the Holy Trinity Monastery in Saharna.

founded in 1776 by the Russian monk Bartholomew. Legend has it that the monk saw a vision of the Virgin Mary on a high cliff, and upon investigation, found her footprint in a rock. That rock, which is preserved in the monastery, attracts Orthodox faithful. The Saharna region is also rich with springs and waterfalls. The Wonderland Spring close by the monastery is believed to be a source of healing waters, and many pilgrims come in search of its miraculous powers.

The Tipova Cave Monastery is built into cliffs that tower high above the Dniester. The monastery includes three religious chambers and monastic cells linked by steps built into the rock face. The oldest of the three chambers, the Elevation of the Holy Cross cave church, dates from the eleventh century.

The Tipova Cave Monastery is built into cliffs above the Dniester River.

The cave monastery at Orheiul Vechi, 31 miles (50 km) north of Chisinau, is located in a large cave high on the bluffs overlooking the Raut River. Built in the thirteenth century, the cave functioned as a church for three nearby villages. With its wide view of the river valley below, the site had great tactical advantages, and Stephen the Great built a fortress there in the fourteenth century. Like many historic churches, the cave complex was closed down during Soviet occupation, and it suffered from vandalism. But today, the frescoes on its interior rock walls have been restored with brightly colored paints and gold leaf.

The Orheiul Vechi Cave Monastery looks out over the Raut River valley.

People attend a religious service at a Russian Orthodox church in Comrat, a city in the autonomous region of Gagauzia.

THE ROLE OF HYMNS

Throughout the centuries, the Orthodox liturgy has been richly embellished with cycles of hymns from a wide variety of sources. In the early centuries of the church, Christians sang in unison. The music was never written down but simply transmitted orally. It was not until the third century that a system of church melodies was put together. The use of instruments in Christian worship was discouraged by the early church fathers, as they felt that the instruments distracted the mind from thoughts of God and turned them toward the self. The Book of Psalms played a central role in early Christian worship, and in the East, the method of chanting the psalms was well established by the end of the fourth century.

MONASTERIES

As in the rest of Eastern Europe, monasteries play a vital role in Moldova. Apart from their purely spiritual work, they are major centers of education. In particular, monasteries have recorded in their chronicles all the major historical events. They have also translated various theological, historical, and literary works into the Romanian language.

Capriana, 22 miles (35 km) northwest of Chisinau, is the site of a celebrated fourteenth-century monastery. Next to the old monastery, which has silver towers reaching to the high dome, is a new church with beautiful paintings that are slowly being restored.

The interior of the Capriana Monastery cathedral is richly decorated in the Orthodox style.

INTERNET LINKS

http://www.bbc.co.uk/religion/religions/christianity/subdivisions/easternorthodox_1.shtml
This site explains how Eastern Orthodox Christianity differs from Catholicism and Protestantism.

http://en.mitropolia.md
This is the official site of the Orthodox Church of Moldova, presented in English.

A landmark sign announces the boundary of the city of Chisinau. It uses the diacritic marks that are part of their alphabet.

9

W HAT LANGUAGE DO THE PEOPLE of Moldova speak? Is it Moldovan? Many Moldovans would say yes. But is Moldovan an actual language? Or is it really Romanian in disguise?

The question is not as strange as it might seem. In 2013, the Moldovan Constitutional Court ruled that the nation's language should be called Romanian, not Moldovan. Linguistically, there's no argument. Linguists worldwide agree that Romanian and Moldovan are one language (not unlike British English and American English). How it came to be divided into two supposedly different languages is yet another example of the intervention of Soviet Russia into Moldova's culture and sense of identity.

Today the Moldovan/Romanian language is a symbol of national pride and cultural heritage—so much so, in fact, that the country celebrates a national holiday in its honor, Limba Noastra (Our Language Day) on August 31.

For centuries, when Moldova was part of the Russian Empire, Russian was the official means of communication. During Soviet rule, Russian was the official language of the Soviet Socialist Republic of Moldavia, as the country was then called. But after the country became independent, it changed its name to Moldova and, in 1994, announced that the state language was Moldovan. Today, just about everyone in Moldova speaks Moldovan ... or rather, Romanian. That is, except in Transnistria, where Russian is still the main language and the Cyrillic alphabet is used. Yet another language in Moldova is spoken by the Gagauz people. There are also local dialects heard in rural parts of the country.

Most people of Moldova are multilingual to some degree. This is because of the country's complex political and social history. Like many other regions of dissolved empires, Moldova is distinctively multiethnic in character. It is this historical complexity that has created an ambiguity in the identity of its people. National and language identities have been hotly disputed and contested in all nation-building debates.

DEVELOPMENT OF MOLDOVAN

The Moldovan language can be traced back to Roman times. When the present-day Romanian and Moldovan territories were conquered by the Romans, the people living there had to adapt to the Roman language and culture. No script existed for "Romanian," the spoken language. The only written languages used in that region were Latin and Old Slavic, but at that time only a few privileged people, such as clerics, scholars, and some noblemen, were able to understand Latin or Old Slavic.

The first known manuscript in the Romanian language appeared in 1420, although it was still written in the Cyrillic characters used for Old Slavic. The actual development of the Romanian written script began in the sixteenth century. At that time, merchants and craftsmen needed a means of written communication to record their trade transactions without being obliged to learn Latin or Old Slavic, and so the Romanian written language was adopted.

LANGUAGE POLICY FROM 1812 TO 1917

In 1812 Moldavia became part of the Russian Empire. The first Romanian school in Moldavia was established by Gheorghe Asachi, who also edited the first Romanian newspaper. In official documents, Moldavian was declared the second national language. Russian was the first.

When Czar Alexander I died in 1825 and Nicholas I came to the throne, the Moldavian people slowly lost their privileges, including their language rights. In 1828, their autonomous status was removed. Moldavians occupying posts in administration were replaced by Russians, the Russian legal and administrative systems were introduced, and Romanian schools were closed. From then until the Russian Revolution in 1917, Romanian could be spoken only in private areas. To pursue a career, knowledge of Russian was indispensable.

THE MOLDAVIAN SOVIET SOCIALIST REPUBLIC

After a short reunification with Romania at the end of World War I, Moldavia then became part of the newly formed Union of Soviet Socialist Republics (USSR or Soviet Union) in 1924. As such, it at first enjoyed a tolerant nationalistic language policy. All ethnic groups had equal rights, and some even received privileges. Their native languages and cultures were promoted, linguists developed written forms of the spoken minority languages, and school lessons were conducted in native languages.

When Joseph Stalin came to power in the USSR, however, he replaced non-Russians and nonconformist Russians in government, administration, and other public positions with his Russian supporters. Russian became the local language, and learning it in school became compulsory. To improve one's social status, one had to learn Russian and adapt to Russian culture. The main aim of Stalin's policy was to deny that Moldavians and Romanians had been one people. Moldavian, he insisted, was a separate language that used the same Cyrillic alphabet that the Russian language used. Romanian, on the other hand, used the Latin alphabet. In written form, at least, the Moldavian and Romanian languages were therefore mutually unintelligible.

After Stalin's death in 1953, the new Soviet leader. Nikita Khrushchev, relaxed these policies, and it became possible again to take part in the cultural life of Romania. Romanian books were sold, and Romanian films were shown. There were even exchange programs organized between Moldavian and Romanian students, enterprises, and theaters.

In the mid-1960s, however, the situation worsened. An anti-Romanian campaign was started, and an emphasis was placed on the independence of Moldavia from Romania. Authors were criticized for Romanian language influences, and Romanian books and films were prohibited from use. Exchange programs were also no longer possible. By the 1970s, the situation improved slightly.

When Mikhail Gorbachev became leader of the USSR in 1985, he implemented a policy of glasnost and perestroika, or "openness" and "restructuring." This encouraged a public opposition movement consisting mainly of writers and linguists who criticized the language policies of the past. In 1988, the Alexe Mateevici Cultural Club was founded. Mateevici, an Orthodox priest who died in 1917, had written a poem entitled "Limba noastra" ("Our Language"). The main demand of this movement and other opposition groups was the promotion of an accurate interpretation of the Moldavian language and history. The protesters campaigned for increased visibility for Moldovan cultural features in public life, abolishment of mixed schools, and the establishment of separate schools for each nation. Mixed schools had parallel classes: Moldavian-Russian, Russian-Ukrainian, and Russian-Bulgarian. During final discussions in Parliament, some five hundred thousand people demonstrated on behalf of the movement.

Two laws were finally passed in August 1989 to revise the language policy and stress the independence of the Moldovan and Russian cultures.

Moldavian was declared the state language to be used in political, economic, social, and cultural life. The intrinsic connection between the Romanian and Moldavian languages was officially recognized. Gagauz became the second state language in areas with a high proportion of Gagauz people, and Russian became the language of communication among the different nationalities. After independence, Moldovans debated whether the name of their language should be changed from Moldavian to Moldovan. The president explained that Moldovan was used in the constitution for political reasons—to lessen the fears of those who opposed imminent reunification with Romania. The public response to the change in name was a resounding "yes."

A man reads a book at a bookshop in Chisinau.

USE OF RUSSIAN BEFORE INDEPENDENCE

The rural population living in villages hardly had any contact with Russians, so there was no need for them to use Russian, which they learned at school. An exception was Moldovan men who had to do military service, since Russian

FREEDOM OF THE PRESS

While press freedom is protected by the Moldovan constitution, the penal code and press laws prohibit defamation and insulting the state. Reporters Without Borders (also known as Reporters sans frontières, or RSF) and Freedom House are two international

nonprofit organizations that monitor freedom of the press around the world. Both have given Moldova dropping scores in press freedom in recent years. In 2017, Moldova rated a status of "partly free," according to Freedom House, and in 2018, it was ranked 81st out of 180 countries by RSF. Both organizations report that Moldova's media is excessively influenced by the country's wealthy business leaders and government officials. As a result, the media is extremely polarized, with some outlets distributing biased content and outright lies.

The media climate in Transnistria is even more restrictive. Authorities, backed by Russia, continue their ongoing campaign to silence independent opposition voices and movements by applying administrative pressure on newspapers and placing restrictions on other media. The authorities frequently deny nongovernmental organizations (NGOs), foreign outlets, and citizens themselves access to information.

was the only official language used by the Red Army, where people of different nationalities served together.

For the urban population, which had a high proportion of non-Moldovans, Russian was a common language. Until 1991, it was the language of everyday life. Speaking Russian in public was unavoidable for the urban population. Even today, most urban Moldovans are familiar with Russian.

THE MEDIA

The state-owned national broadcast outlets include one television and one radio station. In addition, there are nearly seventy TV channels and some fifty radio stations operating, and some four hundred print publications—quite a lot of media providers for such a small market. However, many of these outlets are not economically viable and rely instead on funding from oligarchs and politicians who tend to use them to promote their interests. The Transnistria region operates its own media.

Moldova's leading television station, Prime, carries its own content and rebroadcasts Russia's Channel One as well. Russian TV is popular, but Moldovan officials are wary of allowing too much of it, particularly programs they consider too political or propagandistic in nature. In January 2018, Moldova's pro-Western parliament passed a "media propaganda" law. It bans the rebroadcasting of Russian TV programs on news, analysis, politics, and military issues.

INTERNET LINKS

https://www.bbc.com/news/world-europe-17602346
This BBC News provides a quick overview of the media in Moldova.

https://freedomhouse.org/report/freedom-press/2017/moldova
This is the Freedom House 2017 report on press freedom in Moldova; more recent reports will be available.

https://www.omniglot.com/writing/gagauz.htm
The language of the Gagauz people of Moldova is introduced on this site.

https://www.omniglot.com/writing/romanian.htm
Omniglot offers a good introduction to the Romanian language.

https://rsf.org/en/moldova
Reporters Without Borders reports on press freedom in Moldova; annual reports are available.

ARTS

The National Museum of History is lit up at night.

10

THE ARTS REFLECT A PEOPLE'S history, and that is certainly true in Moldova. The ethnic bonds between Moldovans and Romanians are deeply rooted and reflected in the country's culture. But decades under the Soviet system left their mark as well. Under the Soviets, the government closely directed all artistic endeavors, from painting to architecture to theater, movies, and television. The authorities censored literature and all printed materials, and artists who did not adhere to the appropriate aesthetic and correct ideological message were in trouble.

Every May, Chisinau holds the "Night of Museums." For this festival, museums host special evening events, including theatrical performances, readings, singing, tasting sessions, and other forms of entertainment.

FOLK CULTURE

Soviet rule resulted in many ethnic Romanian intellectuals leaving the country to avoid being killed or deported during and after World War II. With their departure, Romanian cultural influences diminished. Soviet authorities developed cultural and scientific centers and institutions that were filled with Russians and other non-Romanian ethnic groups. The

Dolls in traditional ethnic dress depict a scene of peasant life in rural Moldova.

rural, ethnic Romanian population was allowed to express itself only in folklore and folk art. Although the folk arts flourished, they too were Russified.

Even footwear could be seen as political. For instance, in the traditional Moldovan folk costume, the soft leather Romanian moccasin called the *opincă* was replaced by a boot, which is traditionally Russian. Since independence, the moccasin has made a comeback as part of the national costume, particularly in folkloric dance ensembles.

Folk arts, including ceramics and weaving, continue to be practiced in rural areas. Handmade wool rugs, glass, intricate wood carvings, earth-colored and black pottery pieces, native dress, tablecloths, wooden boxes, and dolls are some examples of the traditional crafts still produced today in Moldova.

MUSIC

Today, rock, jazz, hip-hop, and pop music are as popular in Moldova as they are anywhere. There are many bands and singer celebrities active throughout the country and Europe. Moldova regularly participates in the Eurovision Song Contest, with the band SunStroke Project finishing in third place in 2017 with its hit song "Hey Mamma!" Another well-known Moldovan singer is Nelly Ciobanu. A winner of multiple international competitions, she represented Moldova in the 2009 Eurovision Song Contest. O-Zone was a pop trio dance band that hit it big internationally with the song "Dragostea Din Tei" (informally known as the "Numa Numa" song in the United States). The group's founder, Dan Balan, is also a songwriter and performer on his own, and is the only Moldovan musician to be nominated for a Grammy as co-writer of the Rihanna and T.I. song "Live Your Life."

During the Soviet years, however, contemporary music was banned or discouraged, and traditional folk music and classical music were the preferred

SunStroke Project of Moldova performs in the Eurovision Song Contest in 2017.

A Moldovan fiddle player dressed in the national costume plays at a festival of traditional folk arts in 2018.

styles. Moldova's folk music is much like that found through Eastern Europe, played on accordions, fiddles, and wooden flutes. Traditional instruments also include a hammered dulcimer called a *cimbalon* and a type of wooden panpipe called the *nai*.

Moldova has many prestigious music and fine arts schools. The Academy of Music in Chisinau is one of Eastern Europe's oldest and most distinguished conservatories. Graduates play in the finest symphonies and chamber orchestras in Europe and the United States. The Moldovan Academy Ensemble has performed in European and international competitions and has won many awards for its chamber concerts and renditions of native folk music. The National Philharmonic Society travels widely to other European countries to perform and is held in high regard everywhere it is heard.

SOVIET MODERNIST ARCHITECTURE

About 70 percent of Chisinau was destroyed during World War II, first by a massive earthquake in 1940, and then by air bombardment by Axis forces. It was up to the Soviets to rebuild the city, and the famed Russian architect Alexey Shchusev was assigned to design it. The architect, who was born in Chisinau, worked up a plan from 1947 to 1949 but would not live to see it implemented.

The architectural style of the times was used throughout communist Eastern Europe. It is sometimes called Brutalism or socialist modernism. Although the style was by no means limited to the Soviet sphere, the aesthetic was embraced by the communists. It featured large, heavy concrete buildings designed for utilitarian purposes such as housing for urban masses. In addition, the blocky forms often exhibited a kind of futuristic quality.

In Chisinau, one of the best examples of this style is the State Circus building (right). Built in 1981, the round concrete arena was a top circus entertainment venue with 1,900 seats, making it the largest auditorium in Moldova. In 2004, the building was abandoned and quickly fell into disrepair. It was partially renovated, and a smaller venue within reopened in 2014.

Another Brutalist building that dominates the Chisinau skyline is the Romanita Tower (1986), the highest residential building in the city. The round twenty-two-floor tower has an undulating facade of balconies presenting a "modernistic" vision that many view as outdated today. Although it is still occupied, the Romanita is in a state of great disrepair.

One of Moldova's best known composers is Yevgeni (Eugen) Doga (b. 1937). A younger artist, Patricia Kopatchinskaja, born in Chisinau in 1977, is an expressive violinist well known for her fiery performances.

MONUMENTS AND STATUES

Along the main boulevard in Chisinau is a statue of Grigory Kotovsky. In the 1920s, Kotovski attacked Romania in a series of raids. Today, some Moldovans see him as a Moldovan Robin Hood, whereas others consider him a bandit.

Stalinist blocks and neoclassical buildings can be found along the capital's main boulevard. On one corner of the Great National Assembly Square stands the statue of the legendary Stefan cel Mare, or Stephen the Great, the Romanian prince and national hero. This statue, which was made in 1928, had to be moved several times during World War II to save it from falling into enemy hands. Under Soviet rule, it was transported to a more obscure place in the park. In the 1940s, the Soviets replaced it with a statue of Lenin. After independence,

Grigory Kotovsky rides again, immortalized by this statue in Chisinau.

the statue was brought back to its initial location. In front of the History Museum is a statue of a female wolf, feeding the two founders of Rome, Romulus and Remus. This serves as a reminder of the country's Latin ancestors.

THEATER

Moldova has several professional theaters. Chisinau offers the most choices for theatergoers, but there are many small theaters outside of the capital. Members of ethnic minorities manage a number of folklore groups and amateur theaters throughout the country.

At the major theaters, performances are in Moldovan, except at the Anton Chekhov Drama Theater in Chisinau and the Russian Drama Theater in Tiraspol, both of which perform solely in Russian. The Licurici Republican Puppet Theater in Chisinau performs in both Romanian and Russian.

The Mihai Eminescu National Theater, with its stylish Corinthian columns and pale orange facade, has shows throughout the year, although the month

The Mihai Eminescu National Theater in Chisinau is named for the Moldavian poet.

MIHAI EMINESCU

Mihai Eminescu (1850–1889) represents the pinnacle of Romanian and Moldovan literature and poetry. A national poet in both countries, he wrote poems that evoke the nature and soul of the people. Influenced by the European Romantics, his poetry extols the virtue of solitary reflection and stoicism by an individual when faced with disappointment and failure in personal, and especially romantic, life.

He was born in what was then Ipotesti, Moldavia, but which now is a village in northeast Romania. By the time he was sixteen, Eminescu had published his first poem. Joining the National Theater, he met Veronica Micle, who became the great love of his life. In 1883, he published his masterpiece, Luceafărul, *("Evening Star") which incorporates folklore and mythology with his own philosophy of love. The poet held a number of jobs but continued to write and publish his poetry until he fell ill in 1884. He died in 1889 of disputed causes.*

of March marks the start of traditional music and dance. The National Opera and Ballet Theater is a great place to hear piano and organ concerts, musical performances by local and visiting guests, and time honored ballets such as *The Sleeping Beauty*, *Swan Lake*, and at Christmastime, *The Nutcracker*.

There are also a variety of other theaters—Satiricus, Ginta Latina, Luceafarul, Eugene Ionesco, and Mateevici. The Chisinau Marionette Theater opens its theatrical season in February.

LITERARY TRADITIONS

The oldest original Moldavian manuscript still exists. It was written in 1429. Elaborately calligraphed and illustrated books and manuscripts were produced in monasteries during the thirteenth and fourteenth centuries. They were extremely expensive to produce at that time. When the printing press became common, making books became easier and cheaper. Today, book exhibitions encourage literary exchange and introduce the younger generations to well-known writers of the past. One such exhibition is the ten-day Mihai Eminescu Memorial Days.

INTERNET LINKS

https://www.lonelyplanet.com/moldova/chisinau
This travel site highlights the museums, cathedrals, and other top attractions in Chisinau.

https://www.nytimes.com/2016/08/24/arts/international/wild-child-of-violin-on-a-meteoric-rise.html
The violinist Patricia Kopatchinskaja is the subject of this article.

http://www.romanianvoice.com/mobile/poezii/poeti_tr/eminescu_eng.php
Some of the poems of Mihai Eminescu are provided in English translation.

https://strelkamag.com/en/article/kishinev
"A Guide to the Soviet Modernist Legacy of Chisinau" includes photos of the city's Soviet-era buildings.

LEISURE

Children take a break from roller-skating at a recreational center in Chisinau.

11

LEISURE ACTIVITIES IN MOLDOVA ARE much like they are anywhere else— watching TV, surfing the internet, listening to music, reading, enjoying the outdoors, visiting friends, and engaging in sports. In rural areas, activities tend to center around village life. On weekends, urban Moldovans attend the theater and concerts. For young people working in the cities, weekends provide an opportunity for them to return to their parents' home for a visit.

RELAXING AT HOME

Moldovans love to invite friends and family home for a meal. Friends often stop by a person's house without prior notice, and the reception is always friendly. Sometimes even strangers are welcomed into Moldovan homes. When friends gather, they like to play board games as a way of passing time. Board games also have the advantage of involving the entire family. Among the games, chess is the most popular.

On weekdays, after work, most people spend their time at home watching television or a movie. In the past, there were few program choices, and much of it was for propaganda purposes. Now people have

Since Transnistria is not a recognized nation, the soccer club FC Sheriff Tiraspol must play in the Moldovan league in order to participate in Europe's football matches. The hostility between the Moldovan players and the Transnistrians reveals the lack of unity within the league, especially since the well-financed Tiraspol team regularly outplays its Moldovan counterparts.

more choices on the main television channels. Listening to the radio is also a popular pastime. Despite an increase in television viewers, this other form of entertainment has managed to keep its audience.

CONCERTS AND THEATER

Attending music concerts—whether rock, classical, or folk—and watching plays are popular forms of entertainment for Moldovans. The numerous musical events are a legacy from the Soviets, who frequently had musicians and singers perform in the various factories as a means of keeping the workers happy and satisfied. With enormous government subsidies for the arts, going to the theater was an affordable outing in the Soviet days. Now that such financial support has been eliminated, market forces are in play. The result is a significant decline in concert attendance because few people can afford the high ticket prices.

Performers present a concert of Moldavian folk music in Chisinau.

Going to the movies also used to be a favorite activity among younger Moldovans, since there are many movies in Moldovan and Russian, as well as Hollywood films featuring their favorite movie stars. However, now that it's easy to view movies at home, the cinema is slowly losing its audience.

OUTDOOR PURSUITS

Moldova's climate is ideal for outdoor activities, as the summers are never too

A young woman hikes up a hill overlooking the Raut River at sunrise.

hot, rainfall is sparse, and the winters are short compared with those of other countries in this part of the world. The terrain is limited, with no sandy beaches to play ball on or mountains to climb. Nevertheless, walking in the parks in towns and cities can be very relaxing, and exploring the countryside, coupled with a family picnic by a lake, is a pleasant way to spend the weekend.

Hiking in the heavily forested Codri Hills is an experience that Moldovans especially enjoy in the spring and the fall. The advantage of a small country is that such rural areas are easily accessible to city dwellers.

RURAL ACTIVITIES

Under the Soviet system, free time for young people was strictly monitored, especially in the cities. It was important for them to be doing something productive all the time, such as playing the piano, going to music school, or participating in sports, such as wrestling or weight lifting. Leisure in the rural parts of the country, however, was more relaxed, and children could do what they liked. Leisure activities have not changed much since independence and are still conducted along traditional gender lines. Men occupy their free time with wood carving and perhaps some furniture-making. They may gather in a group while engaging in such activities, so there is a fair amount of chatter and gossip.

Women spend their free time doing embroidery or making dresses and quilts, as being idle is frowned on. These activities are carried out in a group setting, so talking and sharing a joke are part of the enjoyment. Passing on traditional stories that have a moral by word of mouth to younger members of the community is prevalent throughout the countryside. Children love these stories, and it helps to connect them with the history and traditions of their motherland.

SPORTS

FOOTBALL Soccer is called football in most places outside the United States. As in most of Europe, it is unsurpassed as the most popular sport in Moldova. It is played and followed by young and old alike and is actively promoted in school. In the evenings, a group of young men can typically be found playing a friendly game or simply kicking a ball around. Competition is fierce between Moldova's two top teams, FC Sheriff in Tiraspol and FC Zimbru in Chisinau. Teams at the grassroots level, on the other hand, find it a lot harder to survive. Young players are often forced to give up the sport at an early age because of a lack of funding.

There are many sports recreation centers for children. Many sports and activities are available to meet different interests, such as soccer, tennis, swimming, judo, karate, and—for the more intellectual—chess. In Soviet times, these social centers or clubs were owned by the government, but they are now privately owned.

TRANTA The national sport of Moldova is *tranta*, a fast form of wrestling which blends traditional Greco-Roman grappling with lifts and throws. Two opponents battle for two three-minute rounds. Different moves earn certain numbers of points. The first fighter to earn twelve points wins. A wrestler who can lift his opponent aloft wins twelve points and is automatically the winner. In one such lift, called the "shepherd's lift," a wrestler pulls his opponent onto his shoulder as if to flip him over and slam him down. The move is so iconic of the sport that it was pictured on a series of Moldovan postage stamps.

INTERNET LINKS

https://www.menshealth.com/uk/building-muscle/a756450/ the-underdogs-of-olympic-wrestling
This article describes the sport of *trânta*.

https://www.nytimes.com/2012/08/20/sports/soccer/soccer-team -of-post-soviet-transnistria-dominates-moldovan-league.html
Transnistria's soccer team is highlighted in this article.

FESTIVALS

New Year fireworks light up the sky above
the Triumphal Arch in Chisinau.

12

LIKE MANY OTHER ASPECTS OF Moldovan life, holiday customs reveal leftover influences from the Soviet years. In other ways, however, the calendar of festivals and observances represents a break from that past, or a reconnection to an earlier past.

As a predominantly Christian nation, Moldova celebrates the two major Christian festivals of Christmas and Easter. In addition, it has patriotic national days and international observances. In 2019, there were fourteen official days off for national holidays, including Christmas on December 25 and Orthodox Christmas on January 7 and 8.

Since many people still live in the rural countryside, the celebration of traditional festivals continues to survive. There are also many important music, arts, folk, and food festivals throughout the year.

NEW YEAR'S DAY

Most Moldovans now celebrate January 1 as New Year's Day, but it wasn't always so. In everyday matters, Moldovans follow the same Western, or Gregorian, calendar that most of the world follows for civil purposes.

In religious matters, however, the Moldovan Orthodox Church follows the Julian calendar, which predates the Western calendar, and religious holidays are celebrated accordingly. The two calendars are very similar; they follow the same months and days. The Julian calendar, named for Julius Caesar, dates to 46 BCE in Rome. It was commonly used throughout

In 2013, Moldova's pro-Western government officially declared December 25 and January 1 as public holidays in recognition of the growing number of Moldovans who preferred to celebrate Christmas and New Year's according to the Western calendar. The Orthodox Christmas, January 7, would remain a public holiday as well. Pro-Russian opposition communists in the government criticized the ruling.

HOLIDAYS IN MOLDOVA

*Dates in **bold** are official national holidays.*

January 1 . . . . **New Year's Day**
January 7 . . . . **Orthodox Christmas (old style)**
March 1 . . . . Martisor
March 8 . . . . **International Women's Day**
April . . . . Orthodox Holy Week (dates change yearly)
April . . . . **Orthodox Easter Sunday and Monday**
April/May . . . . **Memorial Day/Memorial Easter/Parents' Day (one week after Easter Monday)**
May 1 . . . . **Labor Day**
May 9 . . . . **Victory Day (celebrates victory over Nazi Germany, end of World War II)**
June 1 . . . . International Children's Day
July 29 . . . . Constitution Day
August 27 . . . . **Independence Day**
August 31 . . . . **Language Day (Limba Noastră)**
October (first weekend) . . . . . Wine Festival
October 14 . . . . **Capital Day (public holiday just for Chisinau)**
December 24 . . . . Christmas Eve (new style)
December 25 . . . . **Christmas Day (new style)**

Europe until the new Gregorian calendar gradually replaced it. The new calendar, decreed by Pope Gregory XIII beginning in 1582, was a refinement of the older one.

Today, the Julian calendar runs about thirteen days behind the newer one, and the New Year begins on January 14. The most common celebration is to have friends and family sit down together for a special meal and champagne. After the meal, everyone gathers around the television to watch the countdown to midnight. On New Year's Day—whichever of the two—children go door-to-door singing songs and reciting poems. It is customary to give them small amounts of money or candy.

EASTER

Easter was not an officially celebrated holiday when Moldova was under Soviet rule. Nevertheless, it has always been an important religious event for Moldovans. The celebrations start with Palm Sunday on the Sunday before Easter. This day marks the beginning of Holy Week and recalls the arrival of Jesus into Jerusalem, where the people welcomed him by waving palm leaves. On this day, palm leaves are hung in churches and homes. The following Friday, Good Friday, marks the day of the Crucifixion, and Easter Sunday is a day of joy for Christians because it celebrates Jesus rising from the dead. On Easter Monday, the celebration continues. A week later, on Memorial Easter, or Memorial Day, people visit and pray at the graves of loved ones.

A woman in rural Moldova dyes Easter eggs for the upcoming holiday.

In the Orthodox Church, Easter is usually celebrated about three to four weeks later than Easter in the West. On the Orthodox clerical calendar, Easter usually falls in late April.

SPRING FESTIVAL

The month of March marks the start of Martisor, Moldova's spring festival. The festival marks the rebirth of nature after winter. During this lively festival, classical and folk music predominate. Many special concerts and cultural events are held during Martisor.

The International Music Festival of Martisor is attended by bands and artists from many countries, including the United States, France, Germany, Russia, Romania, and Ukraine. Concerts are held not only in Chisinau but also in all of Moldova's other districts. The festival usually opens with a performance focusing on traditional spring customs. Additional concerts are hosted by the Organ Hall, the National Opera, and the National Philharmonic.

The festival occurs during the time when the traditional custom of honoring women is observed throughout the country. The music festival includes an

A TALE OF TWO CHRISTMASES

Moldovans like Christmas so much they celebrate it twice! That's not the real reason, but the country does officially acknowledge two different dates for the same holiday. Followers of the Romanian Orthodox Church—along with pro-Westerners in general—observe Christmas on December 25, according to the Gregorian calendar. Members of the Moldovan Orthodox Church, which follows the Julian calendar, celebrate on January 7. The two occasions are often called "new Christmas" and "old Christmas" to differentiate them. Some Moldovans are happy to compromise by celebrating twice. Whichever Christmas is celebrated, it is typically spent feasting with family and friends, singing carols, and attending church.

Then there are the people of Ukrainian and Russian ethnicity, many of whom live in Transnistria. Some of them prefer the old Soviet way. They don't observe Christmas at all— the Soviets discouraged religion—but they do exchange gifts around a decorated fir tree on New Year's Eve.

During Moldova's Soviet years, the communist authorities did their best to do away with old Christmas customs and replace them with Russianized traditions. For example, Saint Nicholas—or Father Christmas, the European Santa—was banned, and Ded Moroz (Grandfather Frost) was put in his place. This magical old man with a long white beard brings presents to good children on New Year's Eve. Dressed in furs, he is a character out of Russian fairytales, a snow wizard with roots deep in ancient Slavic mythology. He is sometimes accompanied by his granddaughter, Snegurochka, the Snow Maiden.

Ded Moroz is still very popular in Russia, where he is beloved as an authentic symbol of Russian folklore and history, despite his strong resemblance to the Western Santa. However, after Moldova broke free from the Soviet Union in 1991, many people wanted to rid their culture of all things Russian. Life under the Soviet system had been harsh, and most Moldovans were glad to see it end. Those with Romanian ethnicity wished to embrace their own Christian customs. Many also wanted to look to the West and align with Europe. To that end, Ded Moroz was replaced by Moş Crăciun.

Although today's Moş Crăciun is the spitting image of the American Santa Claus, he also has roots in Romanian folklore. An old myth presents "Christmas" as an old bearded man with supernatural powers. The myth is something of an allegory for the emergence of Christianity, but mixed with pre-Christian traditions. In the Romanian language, which is essentially the same as Moldovan, the word for Christmas is Crăciun *or* Crăciunul, *and* Moş Crăciun *translates roughly as Father Christmas.*

exclusive performance for women, scheduled on International Women's Day. It is attended by Moldovan musicians and fashion houses. Flowers and small gifts are given to all women and girls.

SECULAR HOLIDAYS

On March 8, in honor of International Women's Day, gifts of candy and flowers are given to women. The intent of the holiday is similar to Saint Valentine's Day, but romance is not necessarily present. Gifts are meant to be small and inexpensive and represent friendship and best wishes for the future.

May 1, or Labor Day, was a major event before independence. There were military marches and parades in honor of the workers, and local officials made public speeches. It is still a holiday today, although the military marches have all but disappeared. Moldovans now take the opportunity to go to the countryside, have a picnic, and enjoy the lovely spring weather after a long, dreary winter.

INTERNET LINKS

http://www.balkaninsight.com/en/article/christmas-comes-twice -in-divided-moldova-01-05-2018
This article explains how the country experiences two different Christmastimes.

https://www.timeanddate.com/holidays/moldova
This calendar site provides yearly information on holidays and observances in Moldova.

FOOD

A man harvests an abundance of organic yellow plums in his orchard.

13

MOLDOVAN FOOD IS HEARTY AND earthy. Based on meat, bread, potatoes, and root vegetables, the cuisine is much like that found throughout the Eastern European region. Romanian, Russian, Ukrainian, and Bulgarian influences are all found in the Moldovan diet. Garlic, onions, and herbs are used in the cooking of many dishes.

DAILY MEALS

Moldovans tend to get up early and have a light breakfast, usually some bread or pastry, and then have a hearty lunch. In urban areas, breakfast usually consists of open sandwiches with sausage or cheese, coffee or tea, and fruit preserves. People in rural areas tend to eat a more substantial breakfast of kasha (hot porridge), potatoes, bread, and sheep's cheese.

Lunch is typically the main meal of the day, even for those who are working. An everyday meal begins with a choice of many soups, followed by a main dish of fried meat, baked chicken, or salted or pickled fish. Meat is an important part of the Moldovan diet. Smoked meats are sometimes eaten with fried potatoes and boiled vegetables as accompaniment. Except for salt, bay leaves, onions, and garlic, relatively few seasonings or spices

Many traditional Christmas dishes are based on pork, such as pork *sarmale* (cabbage rolls), ham, *saltison* (pork stomach stuffed with chopped meat), pork-foot *racitura* (jelly), meatballs, sausages, and pork chops. In rural areas, a pig is slaughtered several days before the holiday so there is time to prepare the meats.

are used in the flavoring of food. A lot of animal fat, oil, butter, and mayonnaise are used, and food is often fried.

Rice, stuffed cabbage, cucumbers, and tomato salad are also popular among Moldovans. Cheese is often served as a conclusion to the meal. Casseroles and other baked foods are the favorite foods of most people, appearing often on the daily menu of local restaurants. For dinner, people tend to eat only one course.

Bread is an important staple that is served with most meals; wine is served with lunch and dinner.

FRESH PRODUCE

The rich soil and abundant rainfall in Moldova has resulted in ideal conditions for growing many kinds of vegetables and fruit. Cabbage, potatoes, carrots,

beets, and turnips are common crops. In addition, there are tomatoes, peppers, zucchinis, cucumbers, eggplants, and lettuce.

There are plenty of orchards in the valleys of the Codri Hills. The orchards produce apples, plums, peaches, apricots, and walnuts. In autumn, the bark of the apple trees is wrapped with thick strips of cloth to protect the bark from being eaten by animals. A greater variety of fruit, such as strawberries, cherries, watermelons, raspberries, and grapes, is available in the summer.

Farmers raise pigs, goats, poultry, and sheep throughout the country. Pigs in particular are plentiful, as pork is a popular dish.

Fresh produce and other foods entice shoppers at the historic Central Market in Chisinau.

TRADITIONAL CUISINE

Mamaliga (mah-me-LI-ga), a mashed cornmeal similar to polenta, is the national dish. Traditionally, mamaliga was made in a cast-iron kettle over an open fire

and given to farm workers as a cheap yet filling meal. People sometimes eat it cold for breakfast. Moldovans enjoy mamaliga with stews, stuffed cabbage, and other hearty main dishes. Sour cream and white cheese (like feta) are a typical topping.

Ghiveci (GHEE-vetch) is a popular vegetable stew. *Mititei* (me-tee-TAY) are grilled meatballs made from pork mixed with beef or lamb. Usually cooked outdoors over charcoal, they are eaten as a snack or an appetizer and are sold by street vendors in the cities. *Sarmale* (sar-MALL-eh) consists of cabbage or grape leaves stuffed with rice, meat, and herbs. The filling can be cooked in tomato or lemon sauce. The finished product is often served with cream.

Borscht, a rich-tasting beet and vegetable soup, is a Ukrainian national dish that is a great favorite in Moldova. Yogurt is used to make its texture silky. *Ciorba* (CHOR-ba) is a sour-tasting soup that is traditionally made from the fermented juice of wheat bran. Lemon juice is now used as a substitute to make the sour base.

Brinza (BRIHN-zah), a cheese made from sheep's milk, is cured in brine. It is creamy, rich, and salty, ranging from soft and spreadable to semidry and crumbly.

Common desserts are *placinte* (pla-CHIN-te), which are similar to turnovers or pastry pies, and baklava, a Turkish pastry with crushed pistachios or almonds glazed with thick syrup. The result is an extremely rich and sweet dessert.

TRADITIONAL DRINKS

Homemade alcohol, although illegal, is still prepared in parts of the country. It is extremely potent and requires an acquired taste. Wine and beer are more popular and are legally available. Moldova is well known for its fine cognac and brandy.

Tea is widely enjoyed, but Turkish-style coffee is more common. It's usually consumed black, served in small cups, and is very strong and sweet. Water or sometimes milk accompanies daily meals. Lemonade is a popular choice in the summer.

A little boy clearly enjoys his *placinte*.

WINE

Moldova is one of the most interesting wine areas in Europe, with great potential for growth. Wine has been made in this region since the seventh century BCE.

Barrels of wine roll by appreciative onlookers at a a celebration of National Wine Day in Chisinau.

Moldova lies on the same latitude as the greatest wine-producing country, France, although its wine production is much smaller.

In Soviet times, Moldovan wines were used by the Soviet Union as a source of cheap and readily available alcohol. Today the focus is on improving the quality of the wine rather than producing it in mass quantities. The very best wine is pressed and kept in oak barrels for many years.

RESTAURANTS

Most local restaurants in the main cities serve a basic meal that costs much less than a meal in a Western restaurant. Chisinau has some restaurants with beautiful interiors. Dinner at these formal dining places is more expensive. Some of them have music performances during dinner hours.

There are many ethnic restaurants in Chisinau offering Indian, Mexican, Korean, Chinese, Jewish, and Italian cuisine. Fast-food restaurants sell hamburgers, fries, and pizza.

The interior of a restaurant in Butuceni, Moldova, is decked out in traditional Moldovan style.

INTERNET LINKS

https://lacuochinasopraffina.com/en/moldova-travel-food-guide-trip-moldovan-food-wine-places
This travel guide to Moldova includes many pictures of traditional foods.

https://www.md4ever.com/about/aboutmoldova/food.html
An overview of Moldovan cuisine is provided on this site.

MITITEI

1 pound (450 grams) ground beef and/or lamb
1 lb (450 g) ground pork
2 tablespoons extra virgin olive oil
2 Tbsp water
3—6 garlic cloves (to taste), peeled and crushed into a paste
2 teaspoons baking soda
½ tsp dried thyme
½ tsp red pepper flakes, crumbled
½ tsp paprika (hot or sweet)
1 tsp caraway seed
Salt, pepper to taste

Combine meat, oil, garlic, baking soda, thyme, red pepper, paprika, caraway seeds, and 2 tablespoons water in a large bowl.

Season with salt and pepper and knead until well mixed, wetting hands frequently to help keep mixture moist.

Cover bowl and refrigerate for at least 6 hours or overnight.

With wet hands, roll meat into sausages about 3 inches (7.6 centimeters) long and 1 inch (2.5 cm) thick. Heat a grill to medium heat.

Grill, broil, or pan-fry about 7 minutes per side, or bake at 350°F (175°C) for 15 minutes.

Serve as an hors d'oeuvre or with *mamaliga* and a tomato cucumber salad as an entrée.

MAMALIGA

3 cups (700 milliliters) water
1 cup (160 g) yellow cornmeal (medium
  or coarse grind)
Salt, as needed
3 Tbsp (46.5 g) butter, cut into pieces
Butter or oil, to grease bowls

Butter one large or three or four small (individual size) bowls. Set aside.

Bring the water to a boil in a medium pot and sprinkle in the cornmeal, whisking constantly. Season with salt.

Cook, stirring often with a wooden spoon. Reduce heat if it begins to spatter.

Cook until the mamaliga pulls away from the side of the pot and it is thick enough to hold the spoon straight up. Stir in butter.

Serve warm like mashed potatoes.

Alternatively, pour into prepared bowl(s) to cool. When cool, loosen around the edges by pulling slightly with fingertip away from the edge of bowl. Turn out the mamaliga onto a serving plate. Slice into slabs using fishing line, unflavored dental floss, or similar waxy thread.

Serve with feta cheese and sour cream. Serves 3—4.

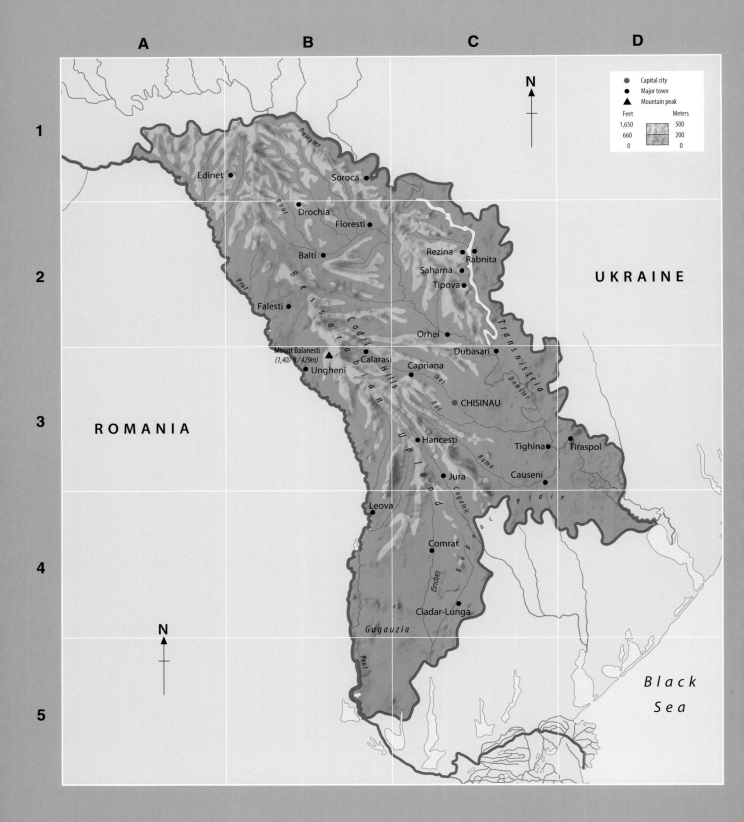

A   **B**   **C**   **D**

N

1

Edinet
Soroca
Dniester

Drochia
Floresti

Raut

2

Balti

Rezina
Rabnita
Saharna
Tipova

Falesti

Bessarabian Codri Hills

Orhei

Dubasari

UKRAINE

Mount Balanesti
(1,407 ft / 429m)
Calarasi
Capriana
Ungheni

Ikel

Bac

CHISINAU

Transnistria
Dniester

3

ROMANIA

Upland

Hancesti

Tighina
Tiraspol

Botna

Jura

Causeni

Plain

Prut

Leova

Cogalnic Botna

4

Comrat

Ialpug Bugeac

Ciadar-Lunga

N

Gagauzia

5

Prut

Black
Sea

	Capital city
	Major town
▲	Mountain peak

Feet		Meters
1,650		500
660		200
0		0

MAP OF MOLDOVA

Bac River, C3
Balanesti, Mount, B3
Balti, B2
Bessarabian Upland, B2—B3, C3—C4
Black Sea, D4—D5
Botna River, C3
Bugeac Plain, C4, D4

Calarasi, B3
Capriana, C3
Causeni, C3—C4
Chisinau, C3
Ciadar-Lunga, C4
Codri Hills, B2—B3, C3
Cogalnic River, C3—C4
Comrat, C4

Dniester River, B1, C1—C3, D3—D4
Drochia, B2
Dubasari, C3

Edinet, B1

Falesti, B2
Floresti, B2

Gagauzia, B4-B5, C4-C5

Hancesti, C3

Ialpug River, C4—C5
Ikel River, B3, C3

Jura, C3

Leova, B4

Orhei, C2

Prut River, A2, B2—B5

Rabnita, C2
Raut River, B1—B2
Rezina, C2
Romania, A1—A5, B2—B5, C5

Saharna, C2
Soroca, B1

Tighina, C3
Tipova, C2
Tiraspol, D3
Transnistria, C2—C3, D3

Ukraine, A1, B1, C1—C5, D1—D5
Ungheni, B3

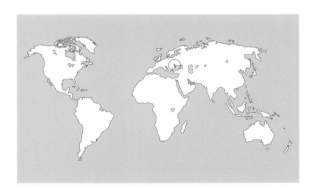

ECONOMIC MOLDOVA

Natural Resources

- Geothermal energy
- Gypsum
- Hydroelectricity
- Lignite
- Limestone
- Phosphates

Manufacturing

- Food processing
- Furniture
- Oil refinery
- Sugar
- Textiles
- Wine

Agriculture

- Cattle
- Fruits and vegetables
- Grain
- Sugar beets
- Sunflower seeds
- Tobacco

Services

- Airport
- Port
- Tourism

ABOUT THE ECONOMY

ABOUT THE ECONOMY
All statistics are 2017 estimates unless otherwise noted.

GROSS DOMESTIC PRODUCT (GDP, OFFICIAL EXCHANGE RATE)
$9.556 billion

GDP PER CAPITA
$6,700

CURRENCY
Moldovan leu (plural lei) (MDL), 1 leu = 100 bani
USD $1 = 17.12 lei (January 2019)

LABOR FORCE
1.295 million

LABOR FORCE BY SECTOR
Agriculture: 32.3 percent
Industry: 12 percent
Services: 55.7 percent

UNEMPLOYMENT RATE
4.1 percent

POPULATION BELOW POVERTY LINE
9.6 percent (2015 estimate)

INFLATION RATE
6.6 percent

NATURAL RESOURCES
Lignite, phosphates, gypsum, limestone

AGRICULTURAL PRODUCTS
Vegetables, fruits, grapes, grain, sugar beets, sunflower seeds, tobacco, beef, milk, wine

INDUSTRIES
Sugar processing, vegetable oil, food processing, agricultural machinery, foundry equipment, refrigerators and freezers, washing machines, hosiery, shoes, textiles

MAIN EXPORTS
Foodstuffs, textiles, machinery

MAIN IMPORTS
Mineral products and fuel, machinery and equipment, chemicals, textiles

MAJOR TRADING PARTNERS
Romania, Russia, Ukraine, China, Italy, Germany, Turkey

CULTURAL MOLDOVA

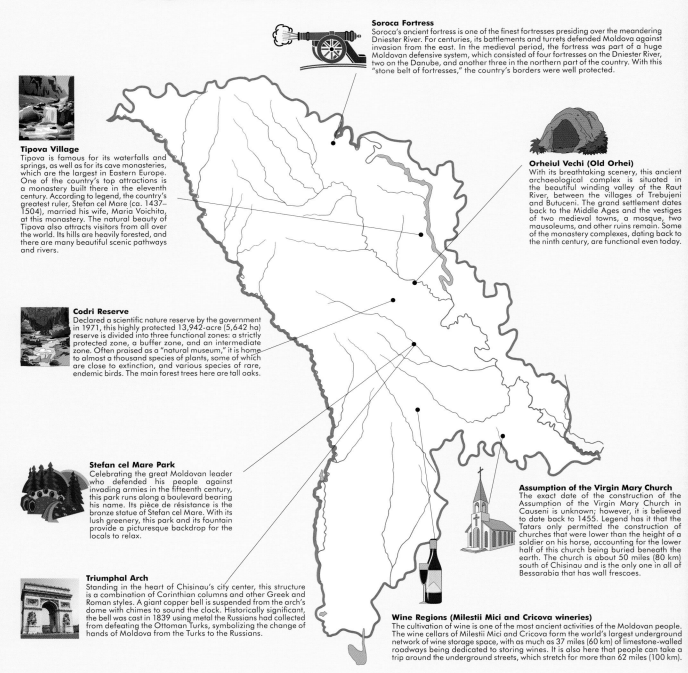

Soroca Fortress
Soroca's ancient fortress is one of the finest fortresses presiding over the meandering Dniester River. For centuries, its battlements and turrets defended Moldova against invasion from the east. In the medieval period, the fortress was part of a huge Moldovan defensive system, which consisted of four fortresses on the Dniester River, two on the Danube, and another three in the northern part of the country. With this "stone belt of fortresses," the country's borders were well protected.

Tipova Village
Tipova is famous for its waterfalls and springs, as well as for its cave monasteries, which are the largest in Eastern Europe. One of the country's top attractions is a monastery built there in the eleventh century. According to legend, the country's greatest ruler, Stefan cel Mare (ca. 1437–1504), married his wife, Maria Voichita, at this monastery. The natural beauty of Tipova also attracts visitors from all over the world. Its hills are heavily forested, and there are many beautiful scenic pathways and rivers.

Orheiul Vechi (Old Orhei)
With its breathtaking scenery, this ancient archaeological complex is situated in the beautiful winding valley of the Raut River, between the villages of Trebujeni and Butuceni. The grand settlement dates back to the Middle Ages and the vestiges of two medieval towns, a mosque, two mausoleums, and other ruins remain. Some of the monastery complexes, dating back to the ninth century, are functional even today.

Codri Reserve
Declared a scientific nature reserve by the government in 1971, this highly protected 13,942-acre (5,642 ha) reserve is divided into three functional zones: a strictly protected zone, a buffer zone, and an intermediate zone. Often praised as a "natural museum," it is home to almost a thousand species of plants, some of which are close to extinction, and various species of rare, endemic birds. The main forest trees here are tall oaks.

Stefan cel Mare Park
Celebrating the great Moldovan leader who defended his people against invading armies in the fifteenth century, this park runs along a boulevard bearing his name. Its pièce de résistance is the bronze statue of Stefan cel Mare. With its lush greenery, this park and its fountain provide a picturesque backdrop for the locals to relax.

Assumption of the Virgin Mary Church
The exact date of the construction of the Assumption of the Virgin Mary Church in Causeni is unknown; however, it is believed to date back to 1455. Legend has it that the Tatars only permitted the construction of churches that were lower than the height of a soldier on his horse, accounting for the lower half of this church being buried beneath the earth. The church is about 50 miles (80 km) south of Chisinau and is the only one in all of Bessarabia that has wall frescoes.

Triumphal Arch
Standing in the heart of Chisinau's city center, this structure is a combination of Corinthian columns and other Greek and Roman styles. A giant copper bell is suspended from the arch's dome with chimes to sound the clock. Historically significant, the bell was cast in 1839 using metal the Russians had collected from defeating the Ottoman Turks, symbolizing the change of hands of Moldova from the Turks to the Russians.

Wine Regions (Milestii Mici and Cricova wineries)
The cultivation of wine is one of the most ancient activities of the Moldovan people. The wine cellars of Milestii Mici and Cricova form the world's largest underground network of wine storage space, with as much as 37 miles (60 km) of limestone-walled roadways being dedicated to storing wines. It is also here that people can take a trip around the underground streets, which stretch for more than 62 miles (100 km).

ABOUT THE CULTURE

OFFICIAL NAME
Republic of Moldova

CAPITAL
Chisinau

MAJOR CITIES
Tiraspol, Balti, Tighina, Ungheni, Soroca, Orhei

NATIONAL FLAG
Three equal vertical bands of blue, yellow, and red; emblem is a Roman eagle, bearing a shield with a stylized ox head.

TOTAL AREA
13,070 square miles (33,851 sq km)

POPULATION
3,437,720 million (2018 estimate)

POPULATION GROWTH RATE
—1.06 percent (2018)

LIFE EXPECTANCY AT BIRTH
Total population: 71.3 (2018)
Male: 67.4 years
Female: 75.4 years

BIRTHRATE
11.2 births per 1,000 population (2018)

INFANT MORTALITY RATE
11.7 deaths/1,000 live births (2018)

DEATH RATE
12.6 deaths per 1,000 population (2018)

ETHNIC GROUPS
Moldovan 75.1 percent, Romanian 7 percent, Ukrainian 6.6 percent, Gagauz 4.6 percent, Russian 4.1 percent, Bulgarian 1.9 percent, other 0.8 percent (2014)

RELIGION
Orthodox 90.1 percent, other Christian 2.6 percent, other or unspecified 7.3 percent (2014)

LANGUAGES
Moldovan, Romanian, Russian, Gagauz

URBANIZATION
Urban population, 42.6 percent (2018)

LITERACY RATE
99.4 percent (2015)

TIMELINE

IN MOLDOVA	IN THE WORLD
1500–1600 CE	
Principality of Moldavia stretches roughly between Carpathian Mountains and Dniester River.	**1530** Beginning of transatlantic slave trade organized by the Portuguese in Africa.
1700–1800	**1789–1799**
Moldavian territory disputed by several powers, with the Ottoman Empire and Russia as the main rivals.	The French Revolution.
1812	
Treaty of Bucharest grants Russia control of eastern Moldavia and the Ottoman Empire western Moldavia.	**1869** The Suez Canal is opened.
1878	
Ottomans recognize independence of Romanian state, including western Moldavia.	**1914** World War I begins.
	1917
1918	Bolshevik Revolution in Russia.
Bessarabia declares independence.	
1924	
Moldavian Autonomous Soviet Socialist Republic established as part of Ukraine SSR.	
1939	**1939**
Romania carved up between Hitler's Germany and Stalin's USSR. Bessarabia goes to the USSR.	World War II begins.
1940	
Russia combines Bessarabia and the Moldavian ASSR to form Moldavian Soviet Socialist Republic.	
1941–1945	**1945**
Following Nazi attack on USSR, a Romanian puppet regime is installed in Moldavian SSR but driven out shortly before the end of the war when the Soviet Union regains control.	The United States drops atomic bombs on Hiroshima and Nagasaki. World War II ends.
	1969 US astronaut Neil Armstrong becomes first person to walk on the moon.
	1986
1989	Era of "openness" introduced in the Soviet Union by Mikhail Gorbachev; nuclear power disaster at Chernobyl in Ukraine
Romanian is reinstated as the official language. The Latin script is adopted to replace the Cyrillic script.	

IN MOLDOVA	IN THE WORLD
1991	**1991**
Moldova declares independence.	Breakup of the Soviet Union.
1994	
New Moldovan constitution grants special autonomy status to the Transnistria and Gagauz regions; declares Moldovan the official language.	**1997**
	Britain returns Hong Kong to China.
2001	**2001**
Communist Vladimir Voronin is elected president.	Al-Qaeda terrorists stage 9/11 attacks against the United States.
2002	
Plans to make Russian an official language spark mass protests.	**2003**
	War in Iraq begins.
2006	
Russian gas giant Gazprom cuts off supplies when Moldova refuses to pay double the previous price.	**2008**
2009	US elects first African American president, Barack Obama.
Vlad Filat becomes prime minister of Moldova when Communists lose their majority. Deadlock over presidency lasts until 2012.	
2014	**2014**
$1 billion disappears from three Moldovan banks, causing major financial crisis. Moldova signs association agreement with the EU. Russia bans Moldovan fruit.	Ebola virus epidemic in West Africa kills at least 11,310 people.
2015	
Former prime minister Vlad Filat is arrested on corruption charges, including the 2014 bank fraud case.	**2015–2016**
	ISIS launches terror attacks in Belgium and France.
2016	
Thousands of anti-government protesters demonstrate in Chisinau, demanding early elections. Moldova's constitutional court rules that presidential elections will be decided by popular vote and not by Parliament. Pro-Russian candidate Igor Dodon wins the presidential election.	**2017**
	Donald Trump becomes US president. Hurricanes devastate Houston, Caribbean islands, and Puerto Rico.
	2018
	Winter Olympics in South Korea. Political crisis in Venezuela continues to worsen.
2019	**2019**
Parliamentary elections in February fail to secure a majority for any party. New elections to be held if ruling coalition cannot be formed within 45 days.	Chinese probe *Chang'e 4* becomes the first human-made object to land on the far side of the moon.

GLOSSARY

baklava
A Turkish pastry with crushed pistachios or almonds.

borscht
A beet soup from Ukraine that has become a Moldovan favorite.

brinza **(BRIHN-zah)**
Sheep-milk cheese cured in brine.

cimbalon
A type of hammered dulcimer used in traditional music.

ciorba **(CHOR-ba)**
A sour-tasting Moldovan soup.

codri
The forest regions of central Molodva.

Gagauz (gah-GAWZ)
A Christian Turkic minority in Moldova.

ghiveci **(GHEE-vetch)**
A popular vegetable stew.

glasnost
The Soviet policy of a more open, consultative government.

judets **(zhu-DETS)**
Counties in Moldova.

leu (plural, lei)
The currency of Moldova.

mamaliga **(mah-me-LI-ga)**
The national dish, made of cornmeal.

mititei **(me-tee-TAY)**
A traditional dish of grilled meatballs.

nai
A type of wooden panpipe used in traditional Molodovan music.

oklad
The decorated metal cover on an icon.

opinca
The soft leather moccasin that is part of Romanian and Moldovan national costume.

pasca **(pas-KUH)**
A yeast bread made at Eastertime.

perestroika
The Soviet policy of reforming the economic and political system.

placinte **(pla-CHIN-te)**
A Moldovan pastry.

Pridnestrovie
The Russian name for Transnistria.

Russification
A process of cultural assimilation in which non-Russian communities, voluntarily or not, give up their culture and language in favor of the Russian one.

sarmale **(sar-MALL-eh)**
Stuffed cabbage rolls.

FOR FURTHER INFORMATION

BOOKS

Ciscel, Matthew H. *The Language of the Moldovans*. Lanham, MD: Lexington Books, 2007.

Hegarty, Thomas, *Moldova*. Postcommunist States and Nations. New York: Routledge, 2003.

Henighan, Stephan. *Lost Province: Adventures in a Moldovan Family*. Totnes, Devon, England: Prospect Books, 2002.

Weiner, Eric. *The Geography of Bliss: One Grump's Search for the Happiest Places in the World*. New York: Hachette Book Group, 2008.

Zlatova, Y., and V. Kotelnikov. *Across Moldova*. Honolulu: University Press of the Pacific, 2002.

ONLINE

BBC News. "Moldova Country Profile." https://www.bbc.com/news/world-europe-17601580.

CIA World Factbook. "Moldova." https://www.cia.gov/library/publications/the-world-factbook/geos/md.html.

Encyclopaedia Britannica. "Moldova." https://www.britannica.com/place/Moldova.

Lonely Planet. "Moldova." https://www.lonelyplanet.com/moldova.

Radio Free Europe/Radio Liberty. "Moldova." https://www.rferl.org/p/5517.html.

MUSIC

Nicolae Bretan: Golem and Arald. Various artists. Nimbus Records, 1995.

Sacred Songs from Moldovia. Ilona Nyisztor. Passion Music, 2006.

Sound the Deep Waters. Izolda. Folk Nouveau Music, 2003.

BIBLIOGRAPHY

BBC News. "Moldova Country Profile." https://www.bbc.com/news/world-europe-17601580

Brownell Mitic, Ginanne. "'Wild Child' of Violin on a Meteoric Rise." *New York Times*, August 23, 2016. https://www.nytimes.com/2016/08/24/arts/international/wild-child-of-violin-on-a-meteoric-rise.html

CIA World Factbook. "Moldova." https://www.cia.gov/library/publications/the-world-factbook/geos/md.html

Economist Intelligence Unit, The. "Democracy Index 2018: Me Too? Political Participation, Protest and Democracy." http://www.nvo.lv/site/attachments/10/01/2019/demokr%C4%81tijas__indekss.pdf.

Encyclopaedia Britannica. "Moldova." https://www.britannica.com/place/Moldova.

Freedom House. "Freedom of the Press 2017: Moldova Profile." https://freedomhouse.org/report/freedom-press/2017/moldova.

Lonely Planet. "Moldova." https://www.lonelyplanet.com/moldova.

Mallonee, Laura. "Meet the People of a Soviet Country That Doesn't Exist." *Wired*, March 7, 2018. https://www.wired.com/2016/03/meet-people-transnistria-stuck-time-soviet-country-doesnt-exist

Montague, James. "In Sliver of Old U.S.S.R., Hot Soccer Team Is Virtual State Secret." *New York Times*, August 19, 2012. https://www.nytimes.com/2012/08/20/sports/soccer/soccer-team-of-post-soviet-transnistria-dominates-moldovan-league.html.

Morar, Margarita. "A Guide to the Soviet Modernist Legacy of Chisinau." *Strelka*, October 25, 2017. https://strelkamag.com/en/article/kishinev.

Necsutu, Madalin. "Breakaway Moldova Region to Open 'Embassy' in Russia." *BalkanInsight*, January 14, 2019. http://www.balkaninsight.com/en/article/russia-is-allowing-a-diplomatic-office-for-transnistria-01-14-2019

Necsutu, Madalin. "Christmas Comes Twice in Divided Moldova." *BalkanInsight*, January 5, 2018. http://www.balkaninsight.com/en/article/christmas-comes-twice-in-divided-moldova-01-05-2018.

Nicoll, Will. "The Underdogs of Olympic Wrestling." *Men's Health*, February 8, 2016. https://www.menshealth.com/uk/building-muscle/a756450/the-underdogs-of-olympic-wrestling.

Radio Free Europe/Radio Liberty. "Moldovan Parliament Speaker Passes Law Against Russian Propaganda." January 11, 2018. https://www.rferl.org/a/moldova-parliament-speaker-approves-russia-media-law/28966975.html.

Reporters Without Borders. "Moldova." https://rsf.org/en/moldova.

Wine of Moldova.com. http://www.wineofmoldova.com/en.

Zveagintsev, Sergei. "Transnistria's Media in Times of Change." Freedom House, August 2018. https://freedomhouse.org/sites/default/files/05%20Transnistria_Eng.pdf.

INDEX

INDEX